D0405501

What Ravi Zacharias and Abdu Murray have done in *Seeing Jesus from the East* is critically needed today. In the West, we've mistakenly believed that Christianity is an outmoded religion. In the East, people see Christianity as a Western religion not meant for them. In highlighting Jesus' Eastern origins and his revolutionary ideas, Zacharias and Murray show that Jesus can appeal to Christians and non-Christians, seekers and skeptics, Easterners and Westerners alike.

LOUIE GIGLIO, pastor, Passion City Church,
and founder, Passion Conferences

As a detective, I learned an important, foundational lesson: avoid presuppositions before beginning any investigation. Years later, when I examined the person of Jesus for the first time, I struggled to shed many of the cultural and skeptical presuppositions I held as an atheist. I wish I'd had Ravi and Abdu's book in those early days of my investigation. They skillfully examine Jesus in his Eastern context and then demonstrate why Jesus matters for both Western and Eastern truth seekers. This book is unique in its genre and a must-read.

J. WARNER WALLACE, *Dateline* featured cold-case
detective, speaker, and author of *Cold-Case Christianity*

Seeing Jesus from the East delivers exactly what it promises—a fresh look at the most influential person of all time. Drawing from their Eastern backgrounds, Ravi Zacharias and Abdu Murray show that the gospel isn't a merely Western message, but one that crosses cultures and even centuries. I highly recommend this book.

ROBERT MORRIS, founding lead pastor, Gateway Church

As an Asian Christian, I have longed to see a book like *Seeing Jesus from the East*. It is seeing Christianity afresh through a non-Western lens, and thus we are wonderfully led to grasp the universal appeal and power of the gospel of Christ, regardless of culture. In a divided world, the unifying and uncompromising message in this book is something we all need.

EDMUND CHAN, founder, Global Alliance
of Disciple-Making Churches

SEEING
JESUS
from
THE EAST

SEEING JESUS

from

THE EAST

A FRESH LOOK AT HISTORY'S MOST INFLUENTIAL FIGURE

RAVI ZACHARIAS
AND ABDU MURRAY

ZONDERVAN REFLECTIVE

ZONDERVAN REFLECTIVE

Seeing Jesus from the East
Copyright © 2020 by Ravi Zacharias and Abdu Murray

Requests for information should be addressed to:
Zondervan, *3900 Sparks Dr. SE, Grand Rapids, Michigan 49546*

ISBN 978-0-310-53128-9 (hardcover)

ISBN 978-0-310-53137-1 (international trade paper edition)

ISBN 978-0-310-11509-0 (audio)

ISBN 978-0-310-53129-6 (ebook)

Published in association with the literary agency of Wolgemuth & Associates, Inc.

Cover design: Studio Gearbox
Cover photo: Serge75/Shutterstock
Interior design: Kait Lamphere

Printed in the United States of America

20 21 22 23 24 25 26 27 /LSC/ 14 13 12 11 10 9 8 7 6 5 4 3 2

*To the memory of our dear friend and
former colleague Nabeel Qureshi.
He wanted so much to write this book with us,
little knowing that his eyes would be seeing Jesus
far better than any book can express.
He is probably smiling at how little we know.*

CONTENTS

PREFACE

Everybody loves a story. Having covered this globe as a speaker for nearly half a century, I have noticed how the posture of a person in the audience changes when I'm telling a story. Actually, this propensity starts early in life. I've seen it both as a father and now as a grandfather. There's never a night with the family that the little children wish to be tucked in without a story. Yet there are different attitudes in the East and the West toward the purpose of a story.

Before my arrival at an Ivy League school in the United States some time ago, there was a lot of back and forth between those who were in favor of my coming and those who were opposed. This was a result of the "new tolerance" in America. I normally don't read any such pro or con sentiment. However, on this occasion, one of my friends sent me an article by a leading atheist on the campus, which he thought would attract my attention.

"Ravi's method is all anecdotal." That was a fascinating statement in the article, and it revealed a mind-set highly conditioned by the Western critical paradigm. The statement bordered on an ad hominem, "against the man," attack but was cleverly camouflaged as a methodological critique. For the sake of civility, I received it as a legitimate criticism and responded in one of my talks. I said, in essence, if I were to ask the writer of that article why he didn't believe in God, chances are one of his strongest reasons would be the problem of evil and the problem of pain. When pushed to justify his reasoning, he would resort to storytelling, using one illustration after another of atrocity or tragedy. Suddenly the stories would become the reason for his disbelief, all while he pretended that the reason made the stories.

What it boils down to is not whether an apologetic is anecdotal or syllogistic, but what place each is afforded in the powers of persuasion. That's the heart of the issue. Both story and argument have a place, and ignoring one or the other risks the extremes of mere illustration or sterile argumentation. What this critic likely didn't realize is that his criticism of my approach, accurate or not, also criticized a whole wealth of Eastern belief systems. Almost the entire sacred text of Hinduism is a story. Much of Islam's hadith are story after story. Buddha's entire authority comes from his story. But where this critic was right is that stories do need a basis for truth-testing before we draw truths from them. That is key. And it is a tough demand.

The amazing thing about the gospel of Jesus Christ is that, though it is a story, it is a story that invites tests for truth. One of the elements that attracted me to Jesus was that everything he said and taught was open to historical investigation and was incredibly supported by prophecies and by his works.

Jesus was the ultimate lawgiver and is the ultimate answer to our struggle to distinguish between truth and lies.

He revealed himself in history and continues to do so in individual lives. He is the supreme doctor, lawyer, philosopher, and healer of the soul.

When I first started to read the Bible, I was surprised by how Jesus regaled his audiences with stories and startled them with unexpected endings. The ultimate surprise was the manner of his death and the power of his resurrection. His stories are so Eastern, and the endings often offer an astounding twist, even for the Easterner. Yet his arguments are also sound for the Westerner.

In this book, my colleague Abdu Murray, a onetime superlawyer with roots in Lebanon, partners with me as we seek to unveil the Eastern face of Jesus. Jesus' Eastern features are undeniable. As you walk this journey with us, you will see that Jesus is never simply Eastern or Western, though, but the Savior of the whole world. Children hover around him, yet teachers of the law are spellbound in his presence. His reasoning is global; his stories are local; his visitation is transcendent; his message is personal; and his implications are eternal.

Join Abdu and me as we take a look at the Eastern Jesus. His message and his method are riveting. In a world skidding out of control, we need him more than ever.

Ravi Zacharias,
Atlanta, Georgia

Chapter 1

A STORY, A FAMILY, AND A SON

RAVI ZACHARIAS

Matthew Arnold penned one of his most noted pieces of poetry in 1853. Nearly nine hundred lines, the epic work is based on another classic piece by the renowned Persian poet Abolqasem Ferdowsi, the *Shahnameh*. In Ferdowsi's narrative, which is really a compilation of stories about Persian kings, the most captivating story is that of Sohrab and Rustum—a father and son. (Note that the latter name is spelled differently, depending on whether one looks at the original or the translation.)

I remember the profound impact this story had on me when I first heard it as a young lad in India. Even the sequence of names caught my attention. Rustum is the father, and Sohrab the son. You would think the father's name would come first in the title. But the story's focus is really on the son and his search for his father.

This is how Arnold's version of the story begins in verse:

And the first grey of morning fill'd the east,
And the fog rose out of the Oxus stream,

15

> But all the Tartar camp along the stream
> Was hush'd, and still the men were plunged in sleep;
> Sohrab alone, he slept not; all night long
> He had lain wakeful, tossing on his bed;
> But when the grey dawn stole into his tent,
> He rose, and clad himself, and girt his sword,
> And took his horsemen's cloak, and left his tent,
> And went abroad into the cold wet fog,
> Through the dim camp to Peran-Wisa's tent.[1]

Rustum is the fiercest fighter in the Persian army. He is revered by those on his side and feared by every opponent. Once, in his younger years, he wandered into another kingdom in search of his lost horse, Raksh. Recognized as a famous, great warrior, he was welcomed by the king.

The young princess also set her eyes on him and, wanting a son from him, offers to return his horse if he will consent to give her a child. Rustum obliges, and before he leaves, he gives her "a clasp which he wore on his upper arm," saying, "If you should bear a daughter, braid her hair about it as an omen of good fortune; but if the heavens give you a son, have him wear it on his upper arm, as a sign of who his father is."[2]

The princess conceives, and by the time her son is born, Rustum is long gone, never to return to her kingdom. The princess sends a false message to Rustum at Sohrab's birth, telling him that the child was a girl so he won't return and try to shape the young Sohrab into a warrior like himself. Sohrab was to be her son and of her making. The princess wanted a son to love, not a warrior to lose.

Yet Sohrab grows up hearing tales of his father and is

determined to find him one day. As he develops great strength and skill in battle himself, his clan ultimately finds itself at war with the Persians. As the story unfolds, father and son finally do meet in a one-on-one fight to the finish, but neither knows who the other is. Locked in hand-to-hand combat, Sohrab suspects he may be face-to-face with the legendary Rustum. Rustum, though much older now, still shows flashes of the prowess he once had. Sohrab doesn't share his suspicions in case he is wrong, but he does not wish to lose to anyone except his renowned father.

Rustum has no inner conflict, as he doesn't even know he has a son. The fight begins, and it is obvious that two of the best warriors in the world are engaged in one of the fiercest fights in history. Only one will be left standing. During a prolonged, multiphase duel, Sohrab finally has the advantage over Rustum, but he holds back from using his sword to finish the fight in case this man is, indeed, his father. Though Sohrab has repeatedly asked, Rustum has refused to identify himself. Finally, the fight turns in Rustum's favor. He has Sohrab on his back and finishes the job. As Sohrab is bleeding to death, he says, "The mighty Rustum shall avenge my death! My father, whom I seek through all the world, He shall avenge my death, and punish thee."[3]

Rustum, stunned, asks Sohrab why he thinks Rustum is his father. With effort Sohrab rolls back his sleeve and reveals the clasp on his arm. Rustum stands speechless and shattered. He has killed his own son, not knowing a son even existed. The warrior is triumphant, but his victory is Pyrrhic. In winning the fight, he has lost something of greater value—he has lost the embrace of his son.

Everything about this story is Eastern. It is a father and son story. A warrior story. A story of killing and power. A mother who does not just bear a child but actively participates in his life and his calling. (You see this same thing in Moses' mother, Jochebed; Samuel's mother, Hannah; John the Baptist's mother, Elizabeth; and Jesus' mother, Mary.) And there is a surprise ending.

There are many such stories in the East, tales of conflict within a family, of power and might, of killing and revenge, of veiling and unveiling—and, yes, of values. In fact, it is the prototypical story of the Middle East to this day. Whether it's the narrative of Islam or the tales of battles in pantheistic religions, this central story is about a war to prove greatness and dominance. It may be fair to say that the tensions between the Sunnis and the Shias started as a succession story. Yet if you look at the key characters in that story, it is a succession story within a family. The whole Sanskrit epic of the *Mahābhārata* is also a fascinating story of a family and the warfare between two brothers.

There is another side to these stories. Many are admittedly mythological, fanciful tales whose details strain credulity. But interwoven within them are philosophical lessons that are meant to provide guiding principles for cultural life. That is the very reason the stories were constructed. In an Eastern pantheistic culture, it is not truth that is the focus, but "truths" that are of importance. Somewhat like Greek mythology, the tales tell lessons. Truths come in proverbs or sayings, seldom in a thought-out, logical framework. Invariably, the writer tells the story as a fable in order to engender some emotion from the reader and to inscribe a timeless principle in the conscience. The story may not be true, but it is intended as a medium of a certain truth.

In Islam, truth *is* important, mainly because it came about as a belief system that claimed to supersede the Christian faith, to which truth is foundational. Muhammad, it is claimed, was the last and greatest prophet. So to Muslims, the story of Islam is a truth claim. Therefore, Islam can and must be tested by its claims.

The gospel of Jesus Christ is also a story. People mistakenly think the story started at Bethlehem, so it's not surprising that critics of the gospel consider it yet another mythological narrative and think they have done away with it. The story of the Father who sends his Son who does his work and returns to the Father may be a beautiful tale, but it cannot be fact, can it?

This is what I assumed when I first read the Gospels without giving them serious thought. I had been to many a Ram Leela performance, as told in Hindu folklore. The play is about Rama and Laxman and Hanuman and Sita, with the bad guy being Ravana, and it is a great battle between good and evil. I never took such narratives to be factual. They were mythological stories meant to teach us to love the values of our culture. So at first blush, my reaction to hearing the gospel was the same; it was just another fanciful tale. That is why I personally studied the book of Romans even before I studied the Gospels. How that came about in itself is interesting.

Shortly after my friend, who is today my brother-in-law, and I committed our lives to Jesus Christ, we were walking by a pile of garbage near our home. Right at the top of the heap was a book with the hard cover open. The title read *Saint Paul's Epistle to the Romans* by W. H. Griffith Thomas. Intrigued, we picked it out of the garbage and began to read it together on our own. To this day, I have no idea who in our neighborhood might have pitched the book into the garbage dump. As far as I know, there was not another Christian in our cluster of friends and neighbors. The book may even have been given to my father by a missionary, as sometimes happened, and my dad, not being a personally committed Christian yet and not knowing better, pitched it into the garbage. As we studied it, we began to also teach it to a group of teens attending a Youth for Christ Bible study. I still have that volume. I treasure it. It was the teaching of what salvation is about that drew my attention, the explanation of the backdrop and implications of the gospel story.

It quickly became evident that the book of Romans is based on the Gospels but goes back to Genesis. Romans explains that one is justified by faith and not by works; it explains what the grace of God and sin mean. This was all so important to the Eastern minds of my friend and me, as well as to the other teens at the Youth for Christ Bible study, because in the Eastern mind-set, the earned liberation of karma is the quest of every individual.

These new gospel categories were real in my experience of salvation, but unknown to me in meditative thought. I knew I was broken inside and the world was broken, but I had never thought about the why and so what of the gospel. The book of Romans, a light that shone into the hearts of Augustine, Luther, Wesley, and scores of others throughout the centuries, shone into my heart too. It is probably the world's greatest treatise on the gospel. The story of the birth, life, death, and resurrection of Jesus is the backdrop, and as I read, I was struck with the thought that the ending was not just a surprise to the reader; it was a surprise even to the gospel writers themselves. That was a huge distinctive from Eastern myths.

Yet the defining difference between the claims of the biblical text and the texts of other faiths is that, right from the beginning, the writers of the Gospels and the Hebrew Scriptures affirm the Bible's stories to be fact, true in detail, a compilation of historic events. That is why Paul illustrates from Abraham. In fact, Paul refers back to Adam, as does Luke. Luke further states, "Since I myself have carefully investigated everything from the beginning, I too decided to write an orderly account" (Luke 1:3). Matthew, writing to the Jews, similarly traces Jesus' story back to Abraham. John connects Jesus' story to the Greeks by using the Greek concept of the *logos*. John states his reason clearly: "But these are written that you may believe that Jesus is the Messiah, the Son of God, and that by believing you may have life in his name" (John 20:31). Belief in the truth and starting "from the beginning"—both of these ideas are writ large in the gospel story.

There are many profound differences between the gospel story and any other story. Though the gospel has elements of an Eastern story, the differences between the gospel and other Eastern stories, between it and Islam, are drastic. These differences create a struggle, propelling us to find a way to understand what is true and why it matters.

MY EASTERN JOURNEY

Let me digress to share a few more personal experiences. My own conversion took place as a pursuit after truth. The search was existential because my struggle was existential. For me, finding enjoyment in sports and competition had been the only real worthwhile pursuits in life. I found life to be its most exhilarating when on the cricket field or the tennis court. (Today, cricket is almost like a religion in India, courtesy of mass communication and big money.)

I seldom gave any thought to religion or spiritual matters, because I never considered the stories I heard to be historically true. They were merely cultural constructs to be transmitted from generation to generation. They provided answers to questions like why family is important, why respect for the elderly is good, why one should never question one's parents, why shame is so devastating, and why the East is superior to the West. Reasons for the latter included that our culture was older and therefore superior; our values in the East were higher than in the West, and therefore we were better; and the morality of the East was better than that of the West, as Christians were bent toward loose living.

We also believed that excellence in academics determines one's future, spirituality is ingrained, and there are powers greater than humanity. Fear of failure and of poverty propelled us to work hard, and superstition controlled all our rituals to that end. Such fear and superstition were systemic within our culture and accepted without questioning. The only time my family ever prayed was when facing a crisis of some sort. The fact that God could be a living, personal being never crossed my mind.

Yet my father would sometimes welcome missionaries who were going door-to-door in the neighborhood into our home as his guests because they were foreigners, and he would ask them to pray with him. I remember laughing the whole thing off, especially when they sang. It was a mean thing to do and terribly immature on my part. My brothers and sisters remember my mockery well.

To even think of absolutes or of God as a real person or a caring entity with whom I could relate was not my focus. Life was about making the best of one's circumstances in one's own interest. It was only when the failure and shame of performing poorly as a student brought me face-to-face with who I really was that I started to ask deeper questions. One of Abdu Murray's chapters ahead expands on this cultural trait. My sense of shame was not based on my own failure alone though. It was also based on my failure in the face of the success I perceived everyone surrounding me experiencing.

These twin realities of my failure and the success of others sank deeply into my soul, beyond surface emotions. It wasn't so much that I feared facing others; it was the anxiety of seeing what lay within me. There simply wasn't meaning in my life. There was a monotony to it and no real destiny to follow. I always thought there must be more to life than what I had; I just didn't know what it was. To put it in the vernacular, not only did I not have a GPS for my soul; I did not even have a destination in mind. To this day, I believe that finding meaning and purpose is the fundamental pursuit of life. Failing to find it has driven many to despair. The book of the Bible that would have resonated most with me at that time would have been the book of Ecclesiastes: everything is vanity.

It was with the fear that there was no purpose to anything I was doing that I attempted suicide at the age of seventeen. There is some perplexity within me today as to why I went that route, because I think so differently now. At that time, it seemed the most pragmatic way to escape my sense of shame. It was in my cultural DNA. When the Bible was brought to me in a hospital room, and I realized the possibility that God might be a real being, for the first time I gave Truth a serious look in the eye. Maybe life wasn't an accident.

WHY THIS BOOK?

When my colleague Nabeel Qureshi asked me several years ago to write this book with him, I resisted because I still think one of the finest texts on the theme of Jesus' Easternness is Kenneth Bailey's *Jesus Through Middle Eastern Eyes*. But Nabeel wanted to present twin views of Jesus from the perspectives of a former Muslim and a transplanted Indian. So we embarked on the project, only to realize within a few weeks that Nabeel would be seeing Jesus face-to-face rather than writing about him. This book is thus dedicated to my dear friend Nabeel Qureshi. My new coauthor, Abdu Murray, and I were both close to him. If you haven't read Nabeel's book *Seeking Allah, Finding Jesus*, may I suggest you do so. It's his story, powerfully told. We became quite close as we traveled together and shared many speaking engagements. Every time I heard him tell his story, I was riveted with a sense of both our common background and the fascinating differences between us.

Nabeel was raised a Muslim in a Pakistani family living in the United States; I was raised in a nominal Christian family living in a Hindu environment in India. Generations ago, my ancestors were devout Hindus from the priestly caste. They would have been well-trained in all aspects of the ceremonies used to access powers of the supernatural and extra-natural. Nabeel's ancestors were Muslim missionaries. They were about converting others to Islam, while my ancestors became converts to Christ. He came from a creedal background; I had no creed.

But there was one thing we shared deeply: our love for our families. That love and a reluctance to bring pain to our parents flowed in our Eastern veins. "If I become a Christian, what will it mean for my family and my culture?" Nabeel feared rejection from his family and culture even more deeply than I did, yet we had common ground for that fear. I feared my father's disdain at my newfound faith, not because of the faith itself, but because of where it might take me professionally. My father considered Christian ministry to be for losers, a view he would deeply regret years later after he made his own commitment to Christ. My family was already an anomaly in a Hindu culture, but a new point of tension existed because now Christianity was not just a general belief I had but a deep, life-changing conviction.

There is a difference between a belief and a conviction. A belief can become something you merely hold; a conviction is that which holds you.

Abdu's story is similar to Nabeel's. His family is Muslim, from a Lebanese background, and he is the only one who has given his life to Jesus. It is tough being the only believer in a cultural context where faith, culture, pride, politics, and law all go together with your family. Departing from your family's faith in Eastern culture is a slap in the face to your ancestors and to your culture as a whole.

Abdu and I both understand the Eastern family well, and one thing stands true: in the East, once you believe something to be true, it is a matter of life and death. That is why my conversion was so dramatic. Finding Jesus to be the Truth was a life-transforming mind-set for me. It was not just turning away from a lifestyle. Unfortunately, it was also seen as a rejection of the culture that cradled me. It took on "traitorous" implications. I remember a Turkish friend with a Christian name telling me that when he would give his name, his Turkish friends would say, "I thought you were a Turk!" The implication was that you cannot be a Turk and have a Christian name. Such a view is ironic, since long before Islam conquered that part of the world, all seven churches in the book of Revelation were in Turkey, yet it is a common Eastern perspective.

My conversion had some of these implications. As a friend of mine used to say, "You have lost your originality," meaning your Christian convictions are not in keeping with your cultural origin.

That assumption is simply not true, but my friend could not see the difference between a mere cultural adherence and a God-given conviction about the meaning of life. My Christian faith became the fortress in which I lived and which I would defend until I died. To this day, I am asked when I meet a fellow Indian, "How did you get a name like Zacharias?" Some think it is a Muslim name, although Muslims generally spell it differently—with a *k* instead of a *ch*.

As a Christian, I embarked on a new journey. I went from

taking life as it came to pursuing what God meant life to be. I had the perspective, as Søren Kierkegaard wrote, that "life must be understood backwards but . . . it must be lived forwards."[4] Truth now mattered. This was the biggest paradigm shift in my life. Culture had its tug and its sway, but my belief in eternal realities had to transcend the headwinds of culture. Jesus was the Truth and the Way. I had needed to find the meaning of life, which Jesus fulfilled. This need for meaning remains the deep battle in the East today, especially with its cyclical view of life and history.

WHAT WAS THE DRAW?

What caught my attention about Jesus' story was not only that it claimed to be true, but also that it was attested to by a collection of writers. What is more, its truth claims reached beyond the characters in the story itself to include all of humanity. Most Eastern sacred texts are written by single narrators. The Bible, by contrast, brings together a confluence of narrators and speaks to our whole cosmos. It offers a *telos*, a purpose-driven story for our existence. Its message is not microcultural, nor, for that matter, a narrative just for *me*. It is not about the superiority of any culture. Instead, it is transcultural, transethnic, and translinguistic. It goes beyond a mere ethical theory or a single language group.

In short, Jesus' story is not a cultural identity story. It is not about what it means to be Indian. It is not about what it means to be in a family, as important as that may be. In its implications and definitions, it is about what it means *to be human*.

The Bible's narrative is the same for *all* mankind. Today in India, you hear the refrain from some that India is a land for the Hindu—Hindustan. "Let's keep India what it is meant to be," they say. What does that statement mean for Muslims, Buddhists, Christians, Sikhs, Jains, and others who have lived in India for generations? Are they implicitly aliens in the land of the Hindus? It can feel that way in India sometimes, not always in social interactions, but when it comes to opportunities for success.

The theologian Paul Tillich said that religion is the essence of culture, and culture is the dress of religion.[5] On the surface, that may sound compelling. But Tillich, like most in his time, didn't envision a world in the transitional stage of becoming multicultural. This is now our reality. This is now our world. Tillich's "essence" and "dress" idea may have been descriptive in his day, but our world of mixed colors and cultures is no longer so simple. When I arrived in Toronto, Canada, in 1966, there were five hundred people of Indian origin living there. Today, there are five hundred thousand in Toronto, and the number is climbing. What is Toronto's culture now? Hardly one essence and one dress.

Imagine if every country defined itself by one religion. All wars would become religious wars, and few passions are as intense as religious passion. Anytime a nation has gone the route of defining itself by a particular religion, it ends up struggling to keep its young people. Often, countries can only do so through fear. Even today, as you enter some Buddhist countries, there are billboards warning that their sacred founder may not be blasphemed against or used as an ornament. We need to do some serious rethinking about ethnocentric, religiocentric cultures.

To bring this point home, ought America to be just for Christians? The whole point of the American experiment was to allow for pluralism without the enforced dominance of one belief. This is a challenge historically for all faiths.

At my first introduction to the message of Jesus, I saw how the Christian faith was not restricted to a single language, unlike Islam's special reverence for Arabic in the so-called genius of the Qur'an. One very quickly recognizes a territorial privilege in language-specific major religions. It is inescapable. Converts to Islam who don't speak Arabic have to learn to say the creed in Arabic. This is a shrewd way to redirect an individual's life, disregarding their language of birth and culture. By learning the phraseology of another language, one becomes identified with another faith. To recognize the "miracle" of Islam, one must understand Arabic. Migration and marriage in Islam also serve to propagate the Muslim faith.

But here's the rub. You can take several divinities out of Hinduism, and Hindu culture holds firm. You can take Muhammad out of Islam, and Allah remains the heart of the Muslim message. Buddha can be an esoteric figure who came and taught and died, but Buddhism remains as a teaching.

You cannot take Jesus out of the gospel story and still have the gospel. No Jesus, no gospel.

It has been rightly said that Jesus did not come so much to preach the gospel but that there might be a gospel to be preached. Sadly, the very name meant to bring salvation has become a name used with crude irreverence and often with profane words, especially in the West. In the East today, it is a name seen as countercultural. Incredibly, it is a name toward which it is impossible to be neutral. The gospel is not meant to provide lessons about life or to be stand-alone fables. It is the true story about Life itself. And it all hangs on a single peg—the person and the claims of Jesus Christ.

As exclusive as the name is for salvation, the Christian faith gives individuals the right to believe or disbelieve, even while the Bible is clear about the eternal consequences of each decision. Belief may not be compelled, but neither can it be reduced. Freedom to disbelieve is clear. Freedom to disbelieve apart from the consequences God has stated is not granted. The defining question of Christianity lies in the question Jesus posed to Peter: "Who do you say I am?" (Matthew 16:15).

"Sohrab and Rustum" is a story about valor. The characters are incidental. The gospel is not a make-believe story about love; it is a true revelation of the God who is love. If God's love is removed from the revelation, the revelation no longer remains, nor does the defining source of love. The two are inseparable, chronologically and logically.

Even though Sohrab and Rustum are fictitious characters, the reader falls in love with the narrative. The story would make a great play. The gospel offers no such sentimental attraction. The critic who thinks it is just another story of valor, teaching a lesson but not necessarily offering a true account, has lost sight of the reason for the message.

So as I write about seeing Jesus from the East, I find myself torn within. In one sense, the gospel *is* Eastern. In another sense, it is so countercultural to the Easterner. For those who understand it, there is power both in its facts *and* in its message. For the one who is immersed in an Eastern culture, the gospel draws them in because it is Eastern, yet pulls them out of their cultural context because it is not restricted to the East alone. Those in the East who live in a familial culture may recognize the less positive aspects of their cultural practices; they can also see how the values of the West have been influenced by Jesus.

We have to understand how much of a struggle an Easterner has in both following the gospel story and accepting its implications, in getting to the heart of Jesus' method without resisting his message. The difference in one's perspective on Jesus is a difference of life and destiny. The gospel is a story. It is a story of the Father and the Son and of the love of God for all of mankind. But it is a story that demands a decision, even at the cost of dividing a family.

The Hindu who states that she is accepting of every faith and only opposes conversion is not showing her whole hand. Hinduism has its exclusive claims as well, as does every major religion. A religion that is all-accepting is systemically contradictory. The Hindu also has a point about evangelism, if conversion is coerced and compelled and deceptively done. Sadly, this has sometimes happened. Coercion also happens in politics, in business, in education, and even in the Hindu culture itself. To threaten a person with reprisals if they convert is its own form of coercion. But a Hindu finds himself at odds with himself if he truly sees in Jesus the Savior no other faith offers. He either has to accept Jesus or deny his cultural claim of being all-accepting.

There is a reasoned exclusivity to every faith, and many faiths are rooted in an ethnicity or nationality. I saw in Jesus a belief above culture and ethnicity, a tie that binds us to something greater than our physical DNA. The implicit cultural or ethnic hierarchy in all Eastern beliefs is absent in the gospel. That is why the key verses in John's gospel read, "For God so loved the world that he gave his one and only Son, that whoever believes in him shall not perish but have eternal life. For God did not send his Son into the world to condemn the world, but to save the world through him" (John 3:16–17).

In these forty-plus words, there is so much to be found. The starting point of the gospel is filial. The gift is unconditional. The reception is personal. The range is eternal. The terms are relational. The core is judicial.

Such depth and breadth could have only come from God. That is why the hymn writer says:

> *In Christ there is no east or west,*
> *In Him no south or north;*
> *But one great fellowship of love*
> *Throughout the whole wide earth.*[6]

THE BEAUTIFUL BREADTH

It's been said, "I like your Christ; I do not like your Christians." That is a fair criticism if one is attacking the hypocrisy in some Christians. I have found the statement is often not just about that though. Many think Jesus never claimed exclusivity but that his followers manufactured this extreme view. Critics similarly attack Christianity as a religion that the apostle Paul invented. Paul did contribute much to our understanding of the gospel; however, he did not develop

Christianity as much as he held it up against the grain of his strong Jewish roots. He saw that the gospel wasn't a message just for the law-abiding Pharisee, which at first irked him. It was not for a privileged class, but for all of humanity. It was not a message such as "Hindustan" for the Hindus. It was a message for the whole world, for all of humanity—every tongue, tribe, and culture. Humanity perverts such a message by seeking to make it sectarian. Jesus "converts" us to embrace the truth that his message is universal.

In Acts 22, when Paul was given a hearing as a Jewish Pharisee to explain his spiritual journey, we read that his listeners heard him patiently until he used one word. What was that one word? *Gentile!* His listeners did not want a universal message.

When I initially read the Gospels and especially the book of Romans, I saw myself for the first time as a valued individual in a larger story, having particular worth but not exclusive worth. I am not today an Indian who happens to be a Christian; I am a Christian who happens to be an Indian. I also saw then that humanity was the object of God's love. He made us, and he pursued us. He reveals his word for all of us. As a Christian I have no choice but to love all humankind. Jesus' truth may be exclusive, but the respect and love he calls us to is not exclusionary.

I am the father of three children. My love is for each of them with none more important than the other. There is an essential worth and a reflective splendor in every individual that comes to us from our heavenly Father. Only God can create a value structure that is both particular and universal for everyone.

Several years ago, I wrote a series of books on imaginary conversations between Jesus and historical personalities such as Hitler or Buddha or Krishna. To make the conversations more relevant, I added a third, fictional character to each one. It made for a fascinating dialogue. I sent one of the books to a friend from the East to critique before the final manuscript went to the printer. He sent back a reply that surprised me. "Jesus I know, and this historical figure I know of, but who is the other person in the conversation?" My response was that I had added fictional characters to each book to incorporate the current context. He was mystified. "But I don't know anything about them or their background," he replied. He then set about writing an imaginary biography of several pages for each of them, which he sent me, saying, "Now rewrite the book with this background information in mind."

His suggestion made perfect sense to me, because people are a product of what has shaped their questions in the first place. And their questions are the product of their experiences. The Bible is replete with examples of such questions. Every participant in a conversation with Jesus, whether it was Nicodemus, a teacher of the law, or the woman at the well who had been shattered by multiple broken marriages, carried a heart-load of their own beliefs and hurts to their questions. That, to me, is what makes the Bible so relevant. My own story has gradually unfolded before my eyes, but I was not brought into being in a vacuum. I was birthed in a context. In one-on-one conversations with people, Jesus showed how absolutes can remain uncompromised, even while discussions are incredibly personal.

The gospel is a story. It is a true story. It is for the world.

It is propositional, with multiple authors telling the same story across vast chasms of time. It is relational. It is general and particular. It celebrates my origin and points me to my destiny. It teaches me to respect from where I came and to respectfully engage those among whom I was raised. I am ever grateful for my Indian roots. I would not trade them for anything. And I must equally respect another who treasures his or her ethnicity. Our backgrounds are not chosen. They are part of God's path for our lives from where each of our journeys begin.

When I started my journey of faith, I did not see then what I see now. I am an Indian married to a Canadian. We have three beautiful children who love both the East and the West. I am part of a team that includes more than ninety speakers with varied accents, all proclaiming one message. It is an amazing tapestry.

I have a seven-year-old grandson. Earlier this year, his teacher asked his class, "If you could be one person in history, who would you want to be?" My grandson wrote, "I would like to be Martin Luther King and fight racism. Thank you for asking."

He understands the message of Jesus and the equality of all people, as well as the respect and graciousness with which we should respond to each other. He understands the message of God's love.

A STRANGE ENCOUNTER

Some time ago, I was visiting a Middle Eastern country when I received a surprise invitation to meet one of the most feared men in the Islamic world, a self-described terrorist who has a lot of blood on his hands. For those who believe in his cause, he is seen as noble. I accepted the invitation and went with three of my colleagues, one of whom is among the most respected Christian communicators in the Arabic world and who played the lead role in our conversation. This colleague is well-qualified to respond with grace to the questions of Muslims. A psychiatrist by training, he is now our lead apologist in the Middle East.

As we began our conversation, he spoke in Arabic to this individual who had brought two others with him. To say that the man had a fearsome countenance would be an understatement. After my colleague spoke for a few minutes, he translated for us non-Arabic speakers what he had just said. He said, "I have just told him, 'There is a fundamental difference between you and us. When you see a person, you see that person as identical with his belief. So if you don't agree with the belief, your answer is to kill that person. When we see a person, we don't see them as identical with their belief. We may not agree with the belief, but we still love the person. We discuss the content of their belief, but we don't hate the person. We cannot kill a person because of their belief. We believe that every human being is created in God's image, and we cannot violate that.'"

Wow! What a starting point! The terrorist agreed he could not distinguish between a person and their belief. If he didn't agree with a belief someone else had, he was obligated to kill that person—even though they shared a common value as people created by the same God—because, in his view, the belief was false and destructive. It was an unforgettable two hours. The terrorist began his aggressive defense of why he proudly holds his view. In fact, he looked at me and said in Arabic, "Your passion makes me want to go for my gun." That was not a heartwarming thought. Later I found out it was an Arabic saying not meant to be taken literally as much as figuratively. I'm not sure that explanation brought much relief when the words came from a killer who proudly defended why he kills! Still, we will be meeting again. I hope we gave him something to think about.

TRUTH CLAIMS ARE NOT ENOUGH

Truth is the bedrock of the gospel. But how does one know something is true?

I recall a university open forum held in Cape Town, South Africa, in which a questioner asked my colleague Michael Ramsden whether Jesus was just another Santa Claus figure, fabricated to represent our hopes and dreams—just like other figures in that genre. Ramsden's answer was brilliant. He quoted the theologian Alister McGrath, who, in response to the same question, pointed out that it was true that a child could grow up believing in Santa Claus but at a certain age come to recognize it was merely fanciful. However, one never hears of a child growing up disbelieving in Santa Claus and then, after reaching adult years, coming to believe in him. That is a strong point. One has to ask why it is that within a generation of Jesus' resurrection, the entire world was being evangelized, and today the followers of Jesus number in greater proportion than any other religious group. If Islam were not an enforced religion, on the other hand, millions of its followers would reject it.

A friend of mine once commented on how amazing it is that two thousand years after Jesus lived, he is still the center of conversations anywhere in the world, as millions still uphold him as the quintessential expression of how life ought to be lived. The enduring power of Jesus is not just happening in the West either, though it has been more shaped by the gospel message than the East. The apostle Thomas went to my homeland of India to evangelize the highest caste of the Hindu priesthood, the Nambudiris, where he paid with his life. The gospel story has been branded the greatest story ever told; in India, Christmas is called "Big Day."

Jesus was a master storyteller, but not of myths, and his own story is the central story of history and of humanity. His is not a story of power or revenge. It is exactly the opposite. He stated that his purpose was to die at the hands of his enemies, not as a martyr, but as a Savior, and to answer the deepest questions of the human heart. "I am the truth" is a remarkable claim. Truth goes beyond the propositional here. It is *incarnational.* Jesus entered the human scene, not to be a hero, but to show us how valuable we are in his sight.

The truth of the gospel is not only incarnational but also *evidential.* I will deal with this aspect further in the next chapter. While it is true that the gospel is a story, it is also an intrinsic argument. The biblical narrative is a very different kind of metanarrative that tackles the core question of why Jesus is the Truth. Mahatma Gandhi may have said more than he intended on this matter when he said, "God is Truth and Truth is God."[7]

Let me reword his statement. Truth is the very nature of

God. In God there is no contradiction. A lie is that which is not in keeping with reality. Truth is that which conforms to reality. That is why the Gospels never present Jesus merely as a teacher. He is, instead, himself the core of his teaching. Imagine a room full of babies with serious deformities into which a baby perfect in every feature is brought. The gospel at its heart offers a blueprint in Jesus for what life is all about and is meant to be. Jesus' story is intertwined with an argument for his nature as truth: "The Word became flesh and made his dwelling among us. We have seen his glory, the glory of the one and only Son, who came from the Father, full of grace and truth" (John 1:14).

THE VOICES IN THE STORY

Before I conclude this chapter, I would like to explore the nature of argument and story as perceived through Eastern eyes. Which one precedes the other in the Bible? From the beginning of the Bible's overarching narrative, it includes the same five voices: the voice of God, the voice of the tempter, the voice of a fellow human being, the voice of the conscience, and the voice of the Savior. Let's take a closer look at each one and what they say about why the Bible's story unfolded the way it did.

> GOD'S VOICE: I give the blueprint; obedience, for your own sake, spells life.
> SATAN'S VOICE: Disobedience to God will provide autonomy and will not spell death. (This is the ultimate lie.)

HUMAN VOICE: I must also involve someone else.
(Sin is seldom a victimless crime. It seeks company for the wrong reason.)

CONSCIENCE: How do I hide from what I have done? (God speaks from within the human heart as well.)

THE SAVIOR: In order to recover what is lost, provision outside of your own capacity is provided.

The Author of the Story—God's Voice

Genesis 1 begins with the words, "In the beginning God created the heavens and the earth. Now the earth was formless and empty, darkness was over the surface of the deep, and the Spirit of God was hovering over the waters."

What is the first thing one notices? The Bible is a story. It does not use "once upon a time" language but it starts with a onetime happening brought about by the God of eternal existence. God is the creator, and there was a darkness about the material world.

The next verse reveals the very first spoken words: "And God said, 'Let there be light.'"

When I read that, coming from India, I think of how critical the wording is. In the East, we use words like *illumination*, *enlightenment*, and so on. Light has long been the symbol of knowing and seeing. For the Hebrews this was also so. You cannot see in the dark, no matter how hard you try. It is one thing to be in the dark in a place where you are otherwise familiar with the surroundings; it is another thing to be in the dark in a totally unfamiliar place.

I recall being in a meeting where several of us were

interviewed by a host. Just before me was a well-known speaker who had become blind some years before. I will never forget one thing she said: "It is a terrible feeling to open your eyes and still be in the dark." You see, the world was framed within the structure of laws. To exist in this world and be ignorant of the light that structure provides is to be in the dark while having one's eyes open, and it leads one into the abyss of chaos.

A humorous story is told of three professionals in a discussion as to whose was the oldest profession. The doctor said it had to be his, because God created Eve out of the side of Adam. "Somebody had to be the surgeon to sew the side back together," said the surgeon.

"Ah," said the architect, "but before that, the Bible says that God framed the world out of chaos. That clearly is an architect's profession."

All along, the lawyer was grinning as he could taste victory. "Who do you think created the chaos in the first place?" he asked.

There is more somber truth than humor in that statement. This is where the voice of God becomes paramount. The Lawgiver knows what the law is and what it is meant to say. God's stipulation is very clear. He tells Adam and Eve what they may eat and what they ought not to eat. Behind his stipulation was the issue of whether he holds final authority. The light of direction on our path is clear, and God alone is God. Yet by eating from the tree of the knowledge of good and evil, humans took upon themselves the prerogative of playing God. God gave us only one prohibition, and we violated it. Our violation of God's authority has grown since then. Now we kill one another in the delusion that each of us is god.

The voice of God is indispensable to our illumination. We need his light. Pantheistic worldviews are abysmally lost, as all depend on reaching some state of "samadhi" or spiritual bliss that qualifies one to utter ultimate realities realized in that state of mind. Who among us qualifies for that?

There is so much emphasis in the East on meditation. The Bible also is rich in meditation, not for the purpose of emptying the mind, but to reflect on God's mind. We cannot look inward and find in ourselves the answers. We think on things that are of him and seek to walk in his light. At its core, pantheistic beliefs are gnostic, attempting to gain inner enlightenment with no one guiding or enlightening the gurus. Virtually every guru who passes away leaves behind a warring group of followers as to who is the legitimate heir to the accumulated treasures.

God has spoken. Therein is our guidance. That is the first unique truth I find in the Bible as an Easterner. There is not just revelation; there is a Revealer. With him one cannot tailor-make one's own faith. Instead, there is one truth, though it must be personally applied. God tells us what we may and may not do.

The Antagonist—Satan's Voice

Then the Bible introduces a second voice. Satan's voice is clearly heard three times in the Bible. Genesis is the first time. It is next heard in Job, and the third time in the temptation of Jesus. What is Satan's ploy? In Genesis, it is planting doubt in the mind of man about God: "Did God really say?" Doubt energizes unbelief.

From planting doubt, Satan moves on to contradiction. God had said, "You must not eat from the tree of the knowledge of good and evil, for when you eat from it you will certainly die" (Genesis 2:17). Satan comes along and says the opposite: "You will not certainly die . . . When you eat from it your eyes will be opened, and you will be like God, knowing good and evil" (3:4–5). His words were a deadly half-truth, as it is possible to define good and evil for ourselves apart from God, but the result is always ultimately death. Satan specializes in half-truths. The basis of all his temptation is for humans to be like God, not in character, but in authority.

After Adam and Eve sinned, the garden with its laws was now occupied by the lawless. That is "the fall." The steepest fall of all is that in playing God, we displaced God and listened to the voice of the one who seeks to own and ultimately destroy our souls.

A story is told of Sir Isaac Newton. Having labored for hours over his scientific postulates, at the close of a day he got up from his desk, and his dog sitting by the desk got up as well. In doing so, the dog knocked over a candle, and within seconds the stacks of paper Newton had worked on that day were in ashes. Newton is reported to have looked at his dog and said, "You will never know what you have done."

Isn't repeatedly doing the same thing that brings about negative results and expecting a different outcome, even though we were continually warned of the results, the definition of *foolishness*? To do so, knowing the results, is either foolish or deliberately thumbing one's nose at God and his authority, regardless of the outcome, just because we can.

The voice of Satan can be heard loud and clear: "You can

and you should do what you want." The same voice sought to provoke doubt in Job's mind toward God. Satan was the source of doubt between humanity and God from the beginning until he met the God-Man, Jesus, and lost the battle.

The Protagonist—The Voice of Humanity

Then there is the voice of our fellow human beings. Eve "took" and "also gave" (Genesis 3:6). It just so happened that it was Eve in the position of eating the forbidden fruit first and then sharing it with Adam. It could just as easily have been the other way around. Either way, disobedience hates to be alone. It loves company. Notice that in nearly every illicit act, there is an enabler or an encourager pushing someone else do the same. Incredibly, while both Adam and Eve clearly participated in the disobedient act, both blamed someone else. Adam blamed God and Eve. "The woman *you* put here with me—*she* gave me some fruit, and I ate it" (3:12, emphasis mine). When it was Eve's turn to speak, she blamed the serpent. There was no one left to blame. All four in the situation had now been implicated by the two who disobeyed.

Deception, disobedience, and disowning responsibility stalk our lives every day. Satan's appeal, "You can and you should," is evident in every seduction. The eyes, the will, the desire for power and autonomy—all come into play. But we seldom fall alone. We usually take others with us. In our days, it is very evident that when sin is desired, it never lacks company. Once upon a time, the tower of Babel was hindered from being built because the Lord said that if all humans spoke the same language, evil would find solidarity. The people of that day were blessed to have the tower fall. Today the internet might be considered our tower of Babel. We can all speak to each other on the internet, and that which can be harnessed for good can also be hijacked for evil. How interesting that we have a new word in our dictionary—*netizens*. It implies no national allegiance, just citizenry of the "net," just being wedded to ideas that clash with ideas. That is what Babel was about; from it we get the word *babble*. The human inclination to companionship in evil is a cancerous force spiritually.

The Watchman of the Soul—The Voice of Conscience

Next in the Bible's story comes the subtlest of voices. Adam and Eve realized they were naked and desperately sought to cover themselves. For the first time, the word *afraid* enters the story. They told the Lord that they heard him and were afraid because they were naked. "Who told you that you were naked?" asked God (Genesis 3:11).

This may be the least taught verse in the Bible. Who told them there was something wrong with being uncovered, after having been disobedient to God? The way we view the human body and its connection to shame changed from that moment on.

The previous verse is preceded by, "Then the eyes of both of them were opened" (Genesis 3:7). Were their eyes not opened before? They were, but in the light of an all-seeing God. Now it was in their own eyes—the eyes of humans playing God. The light was changed into darkness because Adam and Eve's darker instincts had squandered the light. They no longer saw each other as partners but as competitors and objects of gratification or blame. The conscience played a role in their recognition of what they had done, and the same conscience played a role in their attempt to cover it up and hide from God.

Guilt is a real feeling, and it must be so. Remember the scene in *Macbeth* when Lady Macbeth and her husband killed King Duncan? It haunted them like a stain that simply could not be washed away. "Out, damned spot!" was her cry. Pilate also tried to wash away the stain of his decision to crucify Jesus. Washing his hands was simple, but eradicating that mark from history was impossible. Two pieces of timber stand today all over the world, and Pilate is known for what he did. The conscience speaks. It says, "You sinned, and you died."

The Deliverer—The Voice of the Savior

Only one voice is left, and it makes Christianity unique. "You need, and I provide," says the voice of the Savior.

In his poem "The Ballad of Reading Gaol," Oscar Wilde wrote, "Only blood can wipe out blood."[8] Our blood-stained lives need the blood of Christ to purify us again. In the Jewish sacrificial system, an animal's blood was shed by the offender to cover his offense. The blood of Christ was shed by the one who was offended so that the offenders could be covered by his righteousness. This truth stands tall among all the faiths of the world, and Christianity is the only faith that takes sin seriously yet offers hope in perfect grace. Christianity's story is thus complete. There is a law that underlies the world, and the forgiveness of Jesus Christ, foreshadowed right from the beginning, brings the world's story to a glorious climax.

God's plan of redemption for us is illustrated near the end of Genesis in the story of Joseph and his brothers. Joseph tells them that what they meant for evil by selling him into slavery, God meant for good, as Joseph became a source of redemption in delivering them and others from famine as governor of Egypt. Joseph forgave his brothers, and his body was entombed when he died. The gospel story ends with the One who offered forgiveness for all and then walked out of the tomb. The entire exodus story, wherein God rescued his people from slavery in Egypt, foreshadows our redemption earned by Jesus from an enslavement of our own making.

Why is the biblical narrative so Eastern? *It's all about the human family.* Genesis is divided among four personalities— Abraham, Isaac, Jacob, and Joseph. Four generations tell the story of faith and the cost of not following God. As I wrote at the beginning of the chapter, family is everything in the East. You are inseparable from your family, but when familial feuds come, the hate is just as intense as the previous devotion. Eastern stories are invariably about a family in close proximity or violent hostility.

Yet the Bible is also the story of all humankind, not just a single family. All other faiths are about and within families. The Hindu scriptures are about a family feud. Islam's history of succession is as well. Buddha taught and modeled abandoning the family to gain individual enlightenment.

The message of Jesus is individual, familial, and universal. His message allows no one to boast. Instead, it calls all to come to our heavenly Father.

The battle in the Middle East today is about which son of Abraham is the chosen one—Isaac, from whom the Jewish people are descended, or Ishmael, from whom the Arab people are descended. God settles it once and for all. It is *neither* Isaac nor Ishmael. It is God's Son, Jesus, who grants all the grace sufficient to be part of his family. Those who recognize him find the answer. Those who do not recognize him perpetuate the problem.

It was the realization, while on a hospital bed, that I couldn't fix the mess I had made of my life that made me realize how lost I was. The central problem of my life was not really whether I should be a cricketer, as I wanted, or a doctor, as my father wanted. It was what I was going to do with the mess of my own inclinations and failings.

The gospel is a story written by many writers. It is a true story. It is a story for all mankind. It is also a personal story. It is ultimately the only story of true liberation. The hymn writer put it well:

> *Long my imprisoned spirit lay*
> *Fast bound in sin and nature's night.*
> *Thine eye diffused a quickening ray;*
> *I woke—the dungeon flamed with light!*
> *My chains fell off, my heart was free,*
> *I rose, went forth, and followed Thee.*[9]

I have had the privilege of speaking at the famed Angola Prison a few times. There are about six thousand prisoners incarcerated there, more than 80 percent of whom are imprisoned for life without parole. The first time I visited, a group of prisoners led in worship. At the end of the service, I asked the worship leader, "If you don't mind my asking, are you in here for life as well?"

He said, "Yes, sir."

"How does it make you feel that you will never get out of

this place?" I asked, because he seemed so at peace as he led in the worship songs. I knew the life of Christ was in him.

He said, "Sir, if you knew the kind of man I was before I got here, and why I was put in here, you would find out that this is the first time in my life that I am really free. Before I got here, I was a prisoner to hate. My parents think because they are not here in Angola that they are free. Actually, they are in a prison of their own making. I am free because of Jesus. This is now my family here."

I could do nothing better than give him a hug. We were brothers, living by faith in the Son of God.

Each time I have gone back to Angola, I've seen the grace of Jesus revealed in more dramatic terms. While I was being shown around once, I was taken to the execution room for those who are under the death penalty. There is a table just outside the execution chamber with chairs around it where the condemned man eats his last meal. When you sit at the table, you face a painting of Daniel in the lions' den. I was told that the prisoner who painted it wished to express that, even up to the last minute, there is always the hope of deliverance. I looked at the painting and asked, "What if they are not delivered?" The chaplain pointed to another wall with a painting of Elijah riding to heaven on a chariot of fire. "Both were painted by the same artist," he said. "He wanted every person heading to his execution to face death with the hope that, one way or another, God would deliver him."

The gospel has amazing power, even in the heart of someone who faces death for a criminal act. One of the thieves executed beside Jesus on Calvary experienced that power in a remarkable way (see Luke 23:42–43).

Billy and Ruth Graham were buried in coffins made by prisoners in Angola. How utterly amazing that a man who preached the gospel of redemption and true freedom requested that his coffin be built by the incarcerated who had found true freedom within, freed at last by the Savior of the world. My wife and I have made the same request. These prisoners know that this world is not their home and that no coffin could ever be their final destination. Jesus assured us of that. Such is the gospel story.

Chapter 2

THE MESSENGER AND THE MESSAGE

Ravi Zacharias

On Christmas Day 2018, the Indian publication *The Wire* posted an article by Rohit Kumar titled, "How Would Jesus Have Fared Amongst Contemporary Indian Godmen?" Kumar had heard the term *Yeshu Baba* while visiting a jail in the company of a group of children performing a Christmas program for the inmates. At the end of the program, one of the prisoners thanked the children for bringing their celebration of the birth of Yeshu Baba to the prison.

Kumar had already heard other titles for Jesus in Hinduism like "Isa Masih," but he felt this new title sounded more familiar and human. He began to compare Jesus to a contemporary Indian baba, a holy man or sage, asking himself the question in the title of the article: *How would Jesus have fared among contemporary Indian gurus or godmen?* To answer the question, he decided to read the gospels of Matthew, Mark, Luke, and John, which tell the life story of Jesus. He concluded that Jesus didn't fare very well by comparison with Indian godmen.

Kumar observed, for instance, that while the patronage of the wealthy is essential for any baba, Yeshu Baba seemed to show no favoritism to the rich. He pointed to the story in Mark 10:17–31 of the rich young ruler who wanted to follow Jesus, to whom Jesus said, "Go, sell everything you have and give to the poor, and you will have treasure in heaven. Then come, follow me" (verse 21). Kumar commented that a modern-day baba would have leveraged the young man's wealth for his movement rather than pointing out, as Jesus did in verse 25, the incompatibility between wealth and spirituality.

In terms of temple worship, Yeshu Baba did not direct the woman in John 4:21 to any particular place, saying, "God is spirit, and his worshipers must worship in the Spirit and in truth" (verse 24)—a stark contrast to what a modern-day baba would request about where to worship. Yeshu also typically stood with marginalized women of his day (see, e.g., John 8:1–11), treating them as equals and showing them respect and understanding, a clear departure from the attitudes of his day and, to a lesser degree, the attitudes of the modern day. Yeshu further encouraged his disciples in Matthew 6 and 7 to seek forgiveness from each other before making offerings to God, and he emphasized humility and service to others out of sight of anyone's observation.

Kumar reached a surprising conclusion: "Yeshu Baba would have been a disaster as a contemporary Indian godman . . . Pro-service, anti-ritualism; pro-poor, anti-elitism; pro-women, anti-patriarchalism; pro-freedom, anti-orthodoxy; Yeshu Baba's career as a godman would have ended before it began.

"Had he been around," Kumar continued, "he would

have most probably found no traction at all with the rich, the powerful and the religious. He might, on the other hand, have found huge appeal amongst the marginalized, the feminists and the liberal. Who's to say, I might even have become one of his followers."[1]

India, of course, is full of gurus. Many Indians, high and low, revere, respect, and admire their self-attained knowledge and ability to live an honorable life. You can often see the bony figure of an ascetic walking along the side of a road, carrying a staff with a small bag draped on his shoulders. The ascetic's spiritual pilgrimage might go on for days. Often a "holy man," bowl in hand, would knock on the door of our home in Delhi, hoping for an extra portion of rice and dhal (a traditional Indian soup). While their lifestyle is austere, gurus often become mentors for sophisticated businessmen and women and well-educated, highly placed officials.

The teachings of these gurus, or babas, can be shallow or deep. A cynical skeptic once summarized a scenario this way:

I can get you a real following if you follow my advice. Wear either a saffron-colored robe or a spotless white pyjama and kurta [the loose-fitting trousers shirt worn by Indian sages] and take up the lotus position with your eyes closed. Have some ash freshly lining your forehead. I will bring ten friends of mine who will sit in your presence, and all you need to do is come up with about fifteen or twenty one-liners such as, "Your hand must be full but your head empty." "Run and never look back because you give an advantage to the pursuer." "Follow the light wherever it leads, and the prosperity of your shadow will always follow you." Just come up with some "wow" statements. They will be entranced by your wisdom, and the next week each one of them will bring ten friends. Within a year, I can make you a millionaire with thousands of followers.[2]

Such cynicism is often warranted, as many so-called "wise men" prey on the gullible and desperate in India who hunger for answers and meaning in life. Of course, such marketing-oriented versions of mystical thought do a disservice to outstanding Hindu thinkers such as Swami Vivekananda (1863–1902), the Hindu monk whose speech caused a sensation at Chicago's Parliament of World Religions in 1893. He had studied both Western and Eastern philosophy, bringing a level of philosophical sophistication far superior to popular guruism.

From the depths of philosophy to shallow popular practices, much Eastern thought ranges from the highly sophisticated to the crassly commercial. Does it not strike us as strange that the land that has exported yoga and meditation is also steeped in corruption and oppression? Yet we see this tragic juxtaposition around the world, and with every religion. These glaring tensions invite scorn from skeptics and doubt from those seeking reasons to believe.

The claims of Jesus are unique and far surpass the maxims of ethical behavior. They go to the core of life's purpose. In the land of gurus, Jesus is seen as, at best, another guru. But is he? Or is he something else entirely?

One of my friends is a professor at a fine university. Of Jewish stock, he maintains that it is impossible to read the gospel of John three times in a row and not be persuaded of Jesus' extraordinary nature. So I put his challenge to the test and discovered both how profound and how down-to-earth Jesus is.

In Hindi we have an expression to describe a "real" person: *dharti ka aadmi*. It means "a person of the soil." Jesus' message and his understanding heart come through again and again in John's gospel. While Jesus repeatedly claims titles that are proper only when used by God,[3] he is nevertheless of the soil.

Merrill Tenney, the famed biblical scholar, refers to the gospel of John as a story steeped in irony. He suggests that in the story of Jesus, we don't see someone so beyond the realm of our experience that we can't relate. Instead, we see someone who came close to us and to our earthly struggles but still speaks of another kingdom. Tenney comments:

> In the life of Jesus Himself irony is apparent. Although He was virtuous, He suffered all possible indignities; majestic, He died in ignominy; powerful, he expired in weakness . . . He claimed to possess the water of life, and He died thirsting. He claimed to be the light of the world, and He died in darkness. He claimed to be the good shepherd, and he died in the fangs of the wolves. He claimed to be the truth, and He was crucified as an impostor. He claimed to be the resurrection and the life, and He expired sooner than most victims of crucifixion usually did, so that Pilate was amazed.[4]

We must see that Jesus' crucifixion is more than ironic. It was a shocking, indeed numbing, ending for the people who believed him to be the victor. As the thief on the cross said, "Aren't you the Messiah? Save yourself and us!" (Luke 23:39). Given all of Jesus' titles, the Eastern mind naturally expects a different ending. The downward trajectory of Jesus' story, if one stops short of the glorious resurrection ending, is nothing less than a monumental tragedy. If, like his disciples, we walk away after Calvary, we will utter the same forlorn words they expressed: "We had hoped" (see Luke 24:21).

Stories are unfortunately not always read in their entirety. Sometimes we miss the ending. Other times we miss the beginning. Reading the five books of Moses or the historical books of the Old Testament, we see the same pendulum-like swing between triumph and tragedy. The Israelite kings never lived the same pattern, good or bad, one after the other. Sometimes even the godly ones, such as Josiah, ended badly. There is a jagged edge to the reality of the Old Testament. It is the gospel—the story of Christ's advent, teaching, death, and resurrection—that provides the logical end and only lasting hope.

Though we sometimes see an incredibly nuanced similarity between religions, we must not miss the defining differences. For example, the *Bhagavad Gita* is the climax of the *Mahābhārata*, two sacred scriptures of Hinduism. Much like the Old Testament's promise to the gospel's fulfillment, the *Mahābhārata* tells the story while the *Gita* gives the fulfillment. But in the *Gita*, "The Song," while the god Krishna talks of duty and sacrifice, there is no supreme sacrifice (other than the duty to go to war even with your brother). In the Christian gospel, however, the supreme sacrifice of the Savior deals decisively with the war within us.

Tragically, Christ followers too often have watered down this matchless story to transform the Christian message into a "Western faith" of joy, peace, and success. So many of us in the West would rather talk of the Enlightenment or various philosophical movements than about our own walk in the darkness, or of cultural drift rather than our own soul struggles. Yes, when tragedy strikes a celebrity or someone close to us, we tend to doubt God and ask, "Why?" But we dare not probe too deeply, busying ourselves instead with mental health awareness and suicide hotlines, which, while good and necessary, don't get to the heart of the matter.

To be sure, the Eastern mind also asks the same question, but not because it doubts God's existence. Rather, like Job, it wishes to probe the mystery of personal pain and individual struggle. The Bible addresses the individual struggle for meaning largely in the person of Jesus. His answer is not merely in statements but in himself.

One of India's greatest movies is *Mother India*, filmed in 1957. It portrays a family struggling with ever-present pain. Its songs highlight wounded lives in a wounded culture. Some of the lyrics display a struggle with fatalism—others, with survival amidst persecution and death. *Mother India* is this great nation's parallel to *Fiddler on the Roof*, the story of a Jewish family fleeing one home and one pogrom after another to await the Messiah.

John captures this journey by devoting more than half of the book to Jesus' suffering path. A wounded culture finds its best answer in a wounded Savior.

Let's trace who this Savior is.

KNOWING THE AUTHOR

The gospel of John begins much like Genesis, the first book of the Bible: "In the beginning was the Word, and the Word was with God, and the Word was God. He was with God in the beginning. Through him, all things were made; without him nothing was made that has been made. In him was life, and that life was the light of all mankind. The light shines in the darkness, and the darkness has not overcome it" (John 1:1–5).

This passage does not say, "In the beginning was a guru, or a sage, or a baba," which would have been securely in the comfort zone of the Eastern reader of a pantheistic bent. But it would not have addressed his or her spiritual hunger. This passage introduces us to a Teacher who comes as a revelation of God himself.

The concept of revelation is far different in the East. The Hindu scriptures are divided into the Shruti and the Smriti. The first is best described as, "That which was heard," the second as, "that which was remembered." In the Qur'an, the focus is on the one who received the revelation. In Buddhism, the sermons of Buddha form the scriptures. Eastern sages are more gnostic in the sense that they "know." They have "received" knowledge through various means. Whatever technique they have practiced has brought them insight. That is the starting point.

The Bible's focus, however, is not on the one who received the message—the receptor—but on the one who revealed truth—the Revealer, who is also the Embodiment of God incarnate, the culminating revelation. It is not so much "what was heard" or "what was remembered" but who did the revealing and who enabled the receptors to remember. Not even a prophet is the revelation. It is God incarnate himself. "In the past God spoke to our ancestors through the prophets at many times and in various ways, but in these last days he has spoken to us by his Son, whom he appointed heir of all things, and through whom also he made the universe" (Hebrews 1:1–2).

John 1 gives us a fascinating metaphor of "the Word." Somebody said to me once, "It could just as easily have said, 'In the beginning was a thought.'" I answered, "Yes, but even that would presuppose a 'thinker.'" What we have is the metaphor of language and revelation. But notice the shift— God's word, and God *as* Word; God's light, and God *as* light; God as the revealer, and God *as* the revelation; God as the messenger, and God *as* the message. God is a communicating God, and God is a self-revealing God. That is why we have voices right from the beginning of the biblical story, as discussed in the previous chapter. As Francis Schaeffer said, "He is there and he is not silent."[5]

The background is being set. Light, life, and the message of God are within reach. As Jesus will tell his disciples, we are now the intercessors through the ultimate Intercessor (see John 17). His coming was predicted and his life was demonstrably embodied. That life walked and talked and engaged individuals. Some of these encounters appear in John but nowhere else. John tells us he has told them to us so we might *know* who Jesus really is (see John 20:30–31).

During Jesus' arrest, Pontius Pilate asked him a pragmatic and politically nuanced question: "Are you a king?" (see John 18:33). Exposing Pilate's motives, Jesus asked his interlocutor if this was a genuine question or a setup. But then Jesus went on to say, "My kingdom is not of this world . . . Everyone on the side of truth listens to me" (verses 36–37). The goal of Jesus' reign is not geographical conquest. It is not about Hindustan or the House of Islam or a Christian country. The rule of God comes to us as individuals, one by one. We invite his reign; we obey his voice.

Jesus is the focus. Jesus is God incarnate. Jesus brings the miracle of light and life in us because of who he is. In John, the first-person singular is used with reference to Jesus a massive 118 times—more than in the first three Gospels (Matthew, Mark, and Luke) combined. John clearly is telling us that Jesus is more than "Yeshu Baba." He is "Yeshu *Bhagwan*," Jesus *God*. Not merely Jesus Guru; Jesus *Savior*. It is an all-defining difference. Yeshu Baba is a touching and culturally beautiful description, but it does not express the vast difference between a baba and the divine person of Jesus. In the eyes of God, even a guru needs the Savior.

How does John go about unveiling this mystery and mastery of Jesus Christ?

WHO IS HE?

If somebody were to ask me who I am, I would give my name. If he or she were to ask me for more information, I would give my heritage, my vocation, my family background, etc. I would never think of giving myself the prerogative of being a guide to mankind. "I am," for me, is followed by other qualifiers and defines my relationships.

With Jesus it is transcendentally different. For him, the message of each "I am" in John is as deep as it is broad. These incredibly powerful "I am" metaphors expand our grasp of his person and mission.

- "I am the bread of life" (John 6:35).
- "I am the light of the world" (John 8:12).
- "I am the gate for the sheep" (John 10:7).
- "I am the good shepherd" (John 10:11).
- "I am the resurrection and the life" (John 11:25).
- "I am the way and the truth and the life" (John 14:6).
- "I am the true vine" (John 15:1).
- Then the most staggering claim of all: "Before Abraham was born, I am!" (John 8:58).

That last claim motivated Jesus' opponents to kill him. He did not "come" into being. Jesus was claiming that it is impossible for him not to be. He is the eternal "I Am." The child was born; the Son is given (Isaiah 9:6). Yet the Son eternally exists. His coming was not a reincarnation; his coming was the *incarnation*.

HIS TESTIMONIALS—SO THAT YOU MIGHT BE SURE

Lest we miss the point, the gospel of John gives us not only titles, claims, and stories about Jesus' identity; it also provides an intensity of argument. The very ideas of the Logos, the Word—the logic, the concepts—are all connected to reasoning and propositional truth. John offered evidence for Jesus' authority and authenticity because he wanted the reader not just to *believe* but to *know* that Jesus' claims about himself are true. This is not a gnostic "knowing" available only to the few. It is available to all who seek to know the truth.

Because truth is of paramount importance, claims of truth must be supported. The veracity of the message and the messenger is of primary importance. There are at least five witnesses in Scripture to validate Jesus' statements.

1. The witness of his works. The works or the miracles Jesus performed testified to one greater than a mere man. As noted by Nicodemus, "No one could perform the signs you are doing if God were not with him" (John 3:2). It is fascinating that Nicodemus doesn't merely refer to miracles but to "signs"—indicators to those who knew the Scriptures.

Another time, the religious authorities challenged Jesus to provide a sign to prove his authority. He replied, "Destroy this temple, and I will raise it again in three days" (John 2:19). His detractors questioned how something that had taken nearly fifty years to build could be rebuilt in three days. The disciples remembered this too, after he rose from the dead "on the third day" (Luke 24:7–8).

2. The witness of his Father. Jesus' works left his detractors perplexed as they tried to explain away what he was doing. So they switched gears and criticized him for working on a Sabbath. But they were in for a shock when Jesus reached even higher for his authority. In John 5:17, Jesus said, "My Father is always at his work to this very day, and I too am working." In the fourth gospel, Jesus never refers to God as "our Father." It is either "my Father" or "your Father." But "my Father" was clearly a claim that was so personal his accusers said he called God his own Father.

Jesus' clearest affirmation from his Father came at his baptism, when the Spirit of God descended on him as he was praying and a voice from heaven that was heard by others said, "You are my Son, whom I love; with you I am well pleased" (Luke 3:22). In John 8:14–18, Jesus also claims that the Father's authority is his own authority. Their judgments are always in sync, one with the other. God's affirmation of Jesus as his Son and Jesus' many references to God as his Father together demonstrate the uniqueness of Jesus' claim. Even if we refuse to accept Jesus' words about himself, we cannot escape the Father's affirmation.

3. *The witness of the Scriptures.* Although some of the other gospel writers give us more prophecies about Jesus, John gives us at least eighteen references to the Old Testament. These include a variety of texts, ranging from the Pentateuch, the Wisdom literature, and both the Major and Minor Prophets, including a very significant prophecy from Micah 5:2: "But you, Bethlehem Ephrathah, though you are small among the clans of Judah, out of you will come for me one who will be ruler over Israel, whose origins are from of old, from ancient times."

These three "witnesses"—the attestations of Jesus' works, his Father, and the Scriptures—were clearly claimed by Jesus. They are powerful enough. And after the resurrection, two other significant witnesses were added.

4. *The witness of the descent of the Holy Spirit upon the disciples* (Acts 2:1–12)—witnessed by large numbers.

5. *The witness of the sudden boldness of the disciples* (Acts 2:14 and throughout the rest of the New Testament)—demonstrated through the disciples' teaching and conduct.

Those two witnesses round off the objective support of who Jesus was. But we must also look at the subjective evidence. After the death of his son, Yale philosopher Nicholas Wolterstorff commented, "When we have overcome absence with phone calls, winglessness with airplanes, summer heat with air-conditioning—when we have overcome all these and much more besides, then there will abide two things with which we must cope: the evil in our hearts and death."[6]

Jesus helps us deal with these two giants—the evil in our hearts and death. Let us look at the witness of his presence in the life of one who believes in him.

THE WITNESS OF HIS PRESENCE— A SUBJECTIVE APPROPRIATION

From the Eastern point of view, two things immediately stand out from the preceding testimonials. No one ever made such claims of stupendous proportions while bearing the marks of humble humanity. *What is it about Jesus that makes these claims possible?* As I read them, my Eastern mind goes to work. *What do his claims say about* me?

- I am living in darkness.
- I am destined for death.
- I am like a lost sheep looking for my home.
- I read about many bad shepherds.

- I am merely a branch in search of roots.
- I struggle with finding the way; I am often beguiled by a lie; and life simply seems a drudgery one day after the next.
- There was a time when I was not; then there was a time when I came to be.

Just this last point is worth focusing on for a moment.

My mother was a very private person. But after she moved to Canada, she would often talk of her younger days. One time, she told my wife of the time when she had been formally engaged by her parents to a Hindu man from another city. My mother came from a nominal Christian home, so this news came as a surprise. But as the wedding date got closer, no invitations were sent or arrangements made. Finally, the day of the wedding came and went with no ceremony. So my mother mustered the courage to ask her mother what had happened. My grandmother very casually answered, "Oh, that marriage is off; he died of heatstroke some weeks ago when he was riding a bullock cart in his village." This put her daughter, my mother, into a state of shock, even though she had not wanted the marriage.

Now here's an important point for the purpose of our discussion. If the woman who became my mother had instead married that Hindu man, I would never have been born. There would never have been a person with my DNA. This fact impressed on me the inescapable truth that all of us are contingent beings who at one time never existed and for whom the possibility existed of nonbeing. My birth was not necessary. It just happened to be.

But that reality is not true of Jesus. There never was a time when he was not, in his essence. "I am" was his ultimate claim. So if Jesus is who he claims to be, he not only gives me answers; he, in his person, *is* the answer.

THE LONGING FOR LOVE AND THE FEAR OF THE WORD

Everything in the gospel of John points to why the author is called "the disciple whom Jesus loved" (see John 13:21–30; 18:15–18; 19:26–27; 21:7; 21:20) and who in turn loved Jesus. There is a nervousness in India with the word *love*. In an Eastern home, it is common to hear this statement: "My father has never told me that he loves me." This does not mean that love is not there. During my entire life before my mother's death, I never once heard my dad tell my mother he loved her. My sister is married to a former Hindu. When her father-in-law was dying, he experienced a deathbed conversion. At that moment of settling his destiny, he called the family to his side to tell them he had just committed his life to Jesus. Then he asked his wife to come closer, saying to her, "In all the years I have known you, I have never called you my sweetheart, but I want to do that now."

To a Westerner who sprinkles "honey" into every other sentence as he speaks to his wife, this Eastern cultural characteristic is incomprehensible. Aside from young people who are trying to be more open about how they feel, talk of love in India is mostly confined to the movies, where it is given free rein. This theme of love has played hide-and-seek for a long time in the East. We seek it and then hide it.

So to open the Bible and read that God actually loves us is a breathtaking concept that invades an emotionally barricaded culture. Scripture presents a loving Savior who is unafraid to tell us that he loves us and that we can have a loving relationship with our Creator. He defines who he is and sustains his truth claims by evidences that have transcended time. This is the true "Yeshu Baba."

Chapter 3

LOST AND FOUND FOR ALL

—————

Ravi Zacharias

I n Luke 15, Jesus tells three parables, one after the other, about being lost. His audience consists of tax collectors and sinners, both outcasts in the eyes of the religious elite, who are muttering about the company he keeps. The first parable is about a lost sheep, the second a lost coin, and the third a lost son. Notice the progression.

The lost sheep knows it is lost but does not know the way back, so the shepherd goes looking for it.

The lost coin is lost but of course has no awareness that it is lost. The owner of the coin looks all over the house for the lost coin.

Then comes the classic story of the lost son. He knows he is lost, and he knows the way back because he is lost by his own will.

But in the one story of the prodigal son, all three ways of being lost are addressed. There is a treasure that is lost by being squandered. There is an older brother who is lost by not really knowing the love of the father. There is a younger brother who is deliberately lost. But the amazing thing in this story is that while the younger son is still a long way off in a journey to return to his father, the father runs to meet him. He had been watching for his son. The derelict is welcomed home with a huge celebration.

All the Father asks of us is that we want his love. The older son is reminded that the treasure has always been there for him too—he just had to claim it. Both sons had not been aware that they already possessed the greatest treasure of all—the love of the father. Without it, we are truly lost.

The surprises of this story make it a powerful one, uniquely taught and containing a unique claim. It beautifully illustrates the statement Jesus made in John 10:10: "I have come that they may have life, and have it to the full." Those who, say, court the narrow story of their ethnicity, who could be represented by the older son in the parable, eat a meager meal. Those who see the bigger picture, however, feast at a banquet hosted by the God who is both the author of our diversity and the glue of our unity. The great I AM takes who I am and makes me what I was meant to be. I come home to the love of my Father.

THE METHOD OF JESUS' TEACHING

A British comedian named Alan Bennett once said, "You know, Life—Life—it's rather like opening a tin of sardines. We are all of us looking for the key." Then he added, "We roll back the lid of the sardine tin of Life, we reveal the sardines, the riches of Life, therein and we get them out, we enjoy them. But, you know, there's always a little piece in the corner that you can't get out."[1] It's true! We're all looking for the key to life and can't quite get it all out until we understand the full story.

This message we share ought to faithfully reflect our respect for its content. The method we use, however, shows respect for the listener. The second ought never to violate the first. Using ignoble means to convey a noble message is self-defeating. Jesus' message was for the whole world, but his method was clearly Eastern. From his parables to his conversations, Jesus sought to gently open up the heart of the listener. He knew how to pinpoint the real hunger in every life.

As we share Jesus' message, we must attend to his method, which is part of the gospel story. He appealed to reason, to prophecy, and to testimonials. But the centerpiece of his method was *how he told stories*. In my travels around the world, I sometimes speak to the same audiences more than once. Without fail, people tell me that they remember my stories most clearly. The illustrations seal the argument. But it is more than that with Jesus.

He knows my story.

He knows me.

An African American apologist, Lisa Fields, says that Christians need to fashion their arguments for the faith with the diverse histories of their listeners in mind. Fields believes her ministry is filling a gap. "'I realized that [most] of the apologetics books I was reading were written by white men,' she told *Christianity Today*. 'I thought, "A lot of this material wouldn't appeal to a lot of people in black churches because the illustrations aren't relevant, and some of the issues aren't as relevant. There needs to be a bridge builder.""[2]

That interview suddenly turned on a light for me. African American history is a story that has birthed the arguments and questions of African Americans, not the other way around. That is why I believe a typical apologetic text doesn't appeal to many in wounded or subdued cultures.

Suppose I were to package a meal and advertise it as "the best meal you've ever had." If I then choose to add a dessert to the lineup and again advertise the new combination as "the best meal you've ever had," the discerning consumer will grasp that I will resort to any hyperbole to get him or her to buy my product. Sadly, that is frequently how the Christian message has been packaged—and why the Easterner sees himself or herself as buying a Western product. We add layers of appeal, and skeptics can see through it all. Meanwhile, we have ignored people's personal struggles and authentic needs. Their stories need to be understood, not treated as being of no importance by the simple approach of "receive Jesus and all your troubles will vanish and you will be really happy." They listen to our logic and mutter to themselves, *You have a great message but the wrong audience.* To us they say, "You don't understand me." We do not just have a message to share; there is another's story we must understand first. If we don't, that person will never be able to grasp the beauty of God's story.

Jesus, however, is the master storyteller who comprehends my story better than I do. He enters my world understanding my struggles. The woman at the well in John 4 was startled when Jesus told her everything about herself. She had just come to draw water. The beginning of their conversation had seemed so ethnically and religiously contoured, as all the while she was guarding her deepest need. The woman talked in general terms about broader issues, but Jesus brought the conversation down to the particular—to her specific need and the narrower hurt with which she lived.

She had started off by saying, "You are a Jew and I am a Samaritan woman. How can you ask me for a drink?" (John 4:9). In effect, she was saying, "You are from an elite class; what do you know about my need?" Jesus stunned her with his knowledge about her life and what he uncovered for her. Her practical and impersonal questions about where to worship and what bucket he was going to use to draw water dissolved into the reality of what he told her about herself. The shortcoming was not that Jesus didn't have a bucket, she came to realize; it was the deprivation of her shattered life. If he could uncover her malady, was it possible he would even provide a cure?

So often we live behind a mask, afraid to expose our utter unworthiness. Our biggest shock is coming face-to-face with God and discovering that he comes, not merely offering us forgiveness, but that he knows who we really are and still offers us forgiveness. He knows our debt, and he alone has the resources to cover it. This is the story of grace beyond our understanding.

The Samaritan woman leaves her water jar, returns to her town, and says, "Come, see a man who told me everything I ever did. Could this be the Messiah?" (John 4:29). Nathaniel's experience with Jesus was the same, as was Peter's, as was Paul's. Jesus Christ knew their individual stories.

THERE IS A REAL COST

I was a newcomer to the Christian faith when I heard in Delhi one of the most revered missionaries to India, E. Stanley Jones. Jones was in his eighties then, but he spoke for more than an hour without notes. His style of delivery, his depth, and his love for the Indian people were proverbial. Jones authored many books, notably one titled *The Christ of the Indian Road*.

In one of his books, Jones tells of an Indian man highly placed in the government. This official had one roadblock keeping him from accepting the truth of the gospel. He couldn't understand how one person taking on the sins of another can truly bring forgiveness. The substitutionary atonement of Christ troubled him. All that struggle changed, however, after he betrayed his marital trust. His wife, a believer in Jesus Christ, discovered that he was involved in an adulterous relationship and was crushed. The official and his wife began a long, painful journey of coming to terms with this heartbreak. The day finally came when she told this man that she was willing to forgive him. But he could not grasp how, if she truly loved him, it was "so easy" for her to offer this forgiveness. If it had been the reverse, he knew he would have been outraged, finding it impossible to forgive her.

One day the official came home from work much earlier than usual. No one knew he was there. As he walked toward his bedroom, he could hear sobbing. He slowly tiptoed closer and quietly leaned into his room. There he saw his wife on her knees, crying out in agony and pleading with God to help her forget this horrible reality that was tearing at her soul.

Fighting off the weight of this surge of emotion from his devastated wife, the man quickly found a quiet spot of his own. Burying his face in his hands, he gasped for help from God—realizing that the forgiveness he had been given was not without a huge price and deep pain. His wife, whom he had wronged, was bearing the cost of that wrong so that he, the guilty one, did not have to carry its weight. For the first time he saw what Calvary meant and told Dr. Jones, "I now see who my Savior is, and why."

This is the truth of the waiting Savior. He knows your story. He wants you to know his. Jesus' story is a double-sided story—his and ours, with him paying the price to redeem us. Until we know the real pain of sin, we will never find the true joy of forgiveness.

The great messenger and storyteller Jesus understands my story and provides the cure. Thus, like the woman at the well, I can leave the jar I brought with me, filled with the pain and regrets of my life, and return to my life with the spring of everlasting renewal he has put within me.

The story is told of a little seaside town where the fog was sometimes so thick that ships were prevented from making it safely into port. The townsfolk decided to build a lighthouse. On the day that the lighthouse was finished, they celebrated with bands playing, bells ringing, and trumpets sounding. The mayor cut a ribbon to inaugurate the lighthouse. That night, a huge fog descended once again. Two visitors who had attended the ceremony said to each other, "The light shines, the bells ring, the horns blow, but the fog comes in just the same."

They missed the point. The lighthouse was never intended

to keep the fog from coming in. It was designed to guide ships safely into harbor, through the fog. The Son of God came not to keep the fog from descending but to help the human heart see through the fog.

The Bible gives us repeated instances of what it means to really see. In John 9 the disciples ask Jesus a very Eastern question: "Why was this man born blind? Did he sin before his birth or is this the sin of his parents?" Such a belief remains common in the East to this day.

Jesus categorically answers, "Neither . . . but this happened so that the works of God might be displayed in him" (John 4:3). And in the midst of this, Jesus teaches what real sight is all about. To his watching critics, Jesus says, "For judgment I have come into this world, so that the blind will see and those who see will become blind . . . If you were blind, you would not be guilty of sin; but now that you claim you can see, your guilt remains" (verses 39, 41).

We begin to see that Jesus is talking about two kinds of blindness. Our response to the incarnation—the coming of the Son of God in human flesh—is ultimately not about conditions going on outside of us but conditions always occurring inside of us. It has nothing to do with an eternally recurring cycle of births but with two separate births, each of a different kind. The labor in a woman's body signals the arrival of a child. The battle within the heart of the person, best described as being between darkness and light, necessitates a different birth. It is not about land and territory or revenge and killing. It is about who we are *on the inside*.

Jesus' answer to our struggle is not just propositional. It is personal and relational. It is not about which son battles which father, as in the story of Sohrab and Rustum. It is about the battle within my own heart, me against my proclivities. John gets to this truth through stories in which the great centerpiece is the One who is the light. Jesus challenged the idea of repeated births and spoke only of a rebirth that is by the Holy Spirit. This is a dramatic distinction in the pantheistic East. We are not reincarnated through innumerable births until we break the cycle of rebirths. We are born once. The correction for the sin we each bear in commonality with all of humanity is covered by the sacrifice of Jesus and brought about in the new birth he offers. In 2 Corinthians 5:17, speaking of this new birth, Paul writes, "Therefore, if anyone is in Christ, the new creation has come: The old has gone, the new is here!"

We learn all this in a conversation Jesus had with a learned man named Nicodemus.

HOW DO WE KNOW AND HOW DO WE SEE?

In John 3, Jesus meets with Nicodemus, a teacher of the law, who has recognized something supremely different about the works that Jesus is doing. Somewhat like the author of Yeshu Baba, Nicodemus wonders what is different about Jesus, acknowledging that Jesus' works are possible only if God is with him. Nicodemus is beginning to see. Notice, however, that there is a huge difference between God being *with* somebody and that person actually *being God*. At this point, Nicodemus would not even have thought of the latter.

Jesus answers him, "Very truly I tell you, no one can see

the kingdom of God unless they are born again" (verse 3). He does *not* say, "Unless they are repeatedly born." That would have clearly affirmed the Eastern view of multiple rebirths or reincarnation. No, he says "born again"—just once, not again and again. This incredible statement would have given pause to Nicodemus, who asks the obvious question, "How does one get back into his mother's womb?" (verse 4, my paraphrase). Jesus acknowledges that Nicodemus is now approaching the greatest mystery and the greatest miracle. The birth Jesus is talking about is not physical. It is spiritual. This birth is not about being born into an earthly kingdom. It is about a spiritual reality. This birth is not humanly engineered. It is God-designed. If you will, the Holy Spirit is the one who conceives and is also the midwife.

A Chinese doctor named He Jiankui claims to have produced the world's first "gene-edited baby." However, the Chinese government has charged that in pursuit of "personal fame and fortune," he violated state laws in a human "designer baby" scheme. Numerous geneticists have gone on record warning of the start of a "terrifying new chapter" in the manufacturing of humans.[3] An updated report stated with surprise that in an attempt to "make the twins resistant to infection by HIV," their brains may have been "unintentionally altered" and "cognitively enhanced." These "unintended consequences" are raising mind-boggling questions about where we are headed as human beings.[4]

"Genetically edited babies," "enhanced brain capacity," "resistant to HIV"—all of these point to humanity being designed by the will of man. Nearly two thousand years ago, however, Jesus told Nicodemus that the new birth he spoke of was not of the flesh but of the Spirit (John 3:5–8). To accomplish this, God sent his Son. His birth may have been a surprise to humanity, but it was not a surprise to God. "When the set time had fully come," the Bible tells us (Galatians 4:4), God brought forth his Son. This Jesus, through the effectual working of the Holy Spirit, does not change your physical DNA; he changes your spiritual DNA. This is not gene editing; this is a new creature. Born of the flesh, we are controlled by the flesh. Born of the Spirit, we are controlled by the Spirit. So much is stated in this conversation with Nicodemus that the best minds cannot fully plumb its depth. It concerns a "new person," "born again" to "see the kingdom of God"—a new realm. More than that, those who are born again have a new Master.

In the gospel of Matthew, the word *kingdom* is used forty-seven times. In Mark, it is used eighteen times. In Luke, we see it thirty-seven times. John, however, uses the word *kingdom* a mere five times. Clearly, the focus of John is not so much on the kingdom as it is on the King. As I've already stated, "I am" passages and the rule of Jesus within the heart come to the fore in John. This is God establishing his kingdom within my heart. I am not the king. I obey the King.

Once we "see" as he wants us to see, we fully understand that he knows our story, that he reaches us even in our darkest hour. He came to seek and to save the lost, to give us life to the full. He pursues us so that we see ourselves as lost for the first time and can receive the new life he offers. He gives us hope, even in our darkest hour, even in our individual circumstances.

A HEARTRENDING TRAGEDY

Some time ago, a story made the headlines in some Indian and American newspapers. Three children, aged seventeen, fifteen, and fourteen, were spending Christmas in Tennessee far from their parents, who were in India. Their father was a pastor. Two nights before Christmas, close to midnight, the house the children were sleeping in caught fire. All three perished, along with the woman who was their host. The man hosting them was able to escape with his little son, but he couldn't get back in because the fire raged so fiercely that within moments, the house was in ashes. All this man could do was listen to the screams of the four who burned to death. I read the story of the Naik family with great sadness, not realizing I would be drawn close to them in the days ahead.

A few days later, an Indian Christian wrote a pleading letter to our office, asking if I would speak at the funeral of "three young children of a pastor who were killed in a house fire." All of a sudden, the story I had read became more real. Soon I was on the phone with Pastor and Mrs. Naik in India. She could only weep and, in Indian fashion, call me Uncle. She must have repeated this appellation thirty or forty times . . . Uncle, Uncle, Uncle.

What could I say? I knew any words of comfort would seem trite to this devastated mother. The family is part of a nomadic group called the Banjara, from the Indian state of Andhra Pradesh. Her husband, the pastor, told me, "We listen to you on the radio all the time and are so grateful for the way you answer people. My wife is asking how to answer her Banjara friends who are saying, 'Where was your God whom you have served all these years? He has taken your son and daughters in such a painful and sudden fashion!'"

At first I was silent, knowing an argument was not what they wanted. As I asked the Lord for wisdom, I answered, "No one understands your question better than Jesus, because when he was on the cross, he asked the same question of his Father. He knows exactly why you are asking this."

Later, during my message at the funeral, I closed with the following story.

In 1969, Mark and Gladys Bliss, two missionaries to Iran, were driving down a narrow, two-lane road from Tehran to Gorgan. Also in the car were an Iranian pastor, Haik Hovsepian Mehr, his wife, and their six-month-old child, as well as Mark and Gladys's own three children, ages thirteen, eleven, and three. In an instant, Mark was blinded by an oncoming vehicle and plowed into a truck ahead of him. In the horrible wreck, all the Bliss children and the little Hovsepian Mehr boy were crushed, producing a grief that will never be completely outlived.

Some years later, I met Mark and Gladys in London at the home of some dear Iranian friends. Every time I looked into Mark's eyes, I could think of nothing else but this story. I wondered at the pain in his heart, especially because he had been at the wheel during the accident. It was an evening during which what weighed heaviest on the heart was left undiscussed.

In my message recorded for the Naik children's funeral, I closed with a poem that was dear to the Blisses.

> Lord, when we whispered "Yes" to thee
> So many years ago,

The things that lay ahead for us,
You did not let us know.

We said "Yes" in the sunshine
when our hearts were glad and free
And all we knew was that your love
Would guide us through life's sea.

We couldn't fully count the cost,
For how could we discern
The price we'd pay to win the lost
And hasten your return?

But you, Lord Jesus, led the way
Beneath a troubled sky
And time has written in the sky
Our heartache and our cry.

For now we know what was involved
In our eternal "Yes."
Victory's yes means fiery trials,
Living treasures laid to rest.

Yet ringing from our heart of hearts
Is one triumphant chord:
The sweetest of all harmony, we say,
"It's alright, Lord."[5]

No one can read those words without pausing and realizing that there are promises made at high noon that are put to the test at dusk. Pastor Naik's word to me after the funeral was sent through a friend. "Please thank Ravi. His message spoke to my heart." No, there was no argument or explanation. There was instead the story of others who had experienced the same devastation and the story of the gospel that rang with the same echoing cry and answer. We learn the hard way that God's answers are not always propositional. Sometimes they are only heard in our relationship to him and in his presence within us. He conquers not in spite of our pain but through it.

In the East, the story can often be the answer, or at least the context of the answer. But as Westerners know, the witness must not stop there. That is the pursuit laid out for us in the East. That is why the Gospels are followed in the New Testament by the Epistles with its teaching. When two stories converge, the song in the heart follows—the story of God's Son and the story of my own heart. But the new life he brings is just the beginning. We are called to walk in and grow with the truths he wants us to learn.

The prophet Habakkuk in the Hebrew Scriptures saw a lot of national calamities and longed for answers in the midst of them. One of his prescriptions is, "The righteous shall live by his faith" (Habakkuk 2:4 ESV). This faith is not simple credulity or belief. It is an undying trust in the God whose claims about himself are true. Just as God calls us to faith, he models that faith by *his own faithfulness* to us. In Hebrew, "The righteous shall live by his faith," is rightly translated "The righteous person will live by his faithfulness" (NIV). The Greeks focused on faith. The Hebrews focused on faithfulness as an intrinsic part of faith. We cannot separate the two.

That verse from Habakkuk is repeated in the book of Romans (1:17) to the European church, in the book of Galatians (3:11) to the Asian church, and in the book of Hebrews (10:38) to the Middle Eastern church. Augustine carried it to the church in Africa and ultimately to the West. What lies at the heart of faith and the content of that faith became the major teaching of the early church, which owes to the Eastern mind the understanding of faith and its interplay with faithfulness.

Today the Western philosopher tends to mock faith as antithetical to reason. I dare suggest that in the name of intellect, we fight against faith because we fight against faithfulness, placing our faith instead in the material and the momentary. The one who does so understands neither. Faith and faithfulness go hand in hand. Faith has its reasons, and faithfulness is its fruit.

The East talks of individual enlightenment; the West speaks of a philosophical movement, the Enlightenment. The East talks of reincarnation; the West talks of the Renaissance. Jesus bridges these divides by placing a new birth and a new way of thinking within the reach of mankind—both in the locus of one's own soul. But new birth and a new way of thinking don't stay there as a privatized, individualistic "faith." They impact the larger context of culture, springing from the individual heart. Let me be clear: *cultures* are not born again; *individuals* are born again and bring true renaissance within culture. We see with Christ's light because of the new birth he brings within us.

To see or not to see is determined by *to be or not to be*. To be *what*? To be *born again*. That is the work of God in the human spirit through the cross. It is imparted through the resurrection of Jesus Christ.

I have been a guest at a certain hotel several times in the more than thirty years since it opened. Over the years, I have made friends with many who work there. Over those three decades, I talked the most with a particular bellman named Raj. During my last visit, I noticed his absence for the first couple of days. Assuming he was on vacation, I asked one of the employees how long he would be gone and requested that this man please say hello to him for me. The other man said, "Oh, sir, Raj is no more."

I didn't follow what he meant, so I replied, "He doesn't work here anymore?"

"No, sir! He is no more. He died."

This man's eyes told the story. Shocked, I wanted to make sure we were talking about the same person. The bellman was in his late fifties, only a month away from his retirement, during which he planned to enjoy time with his family. So the hotel employees told me the story. My friend had worked the evening shift one day and headed home, had a light dinner, and went to sleep. That was his last night on earth. Cremations are held within a few hours of death in India. So instead of being at work the next day, the bellman was on his own funeral pyre.

That phrase, "he is no more," haunts me. It's a grim statement of nonexistence—a person we once knew no longer exists. Contrast that statement with the Naik family's loss. Pastor Naik told me that among the ashes of his children's room their Bible was found intact. "That was a strong reminder to me," he said, "that God's Word abides forever, and it reminded me that they are not gone. They are with Jesus."

The story of the gospel is the story of eternal life. My life is unique and will endure eternally in God's presence. I will never be "no more." I will never be lost because I will be with the One who saves me. How do I know that? When the women came to the garden tomb looking for Jesus' body, they were met by an angel, who said, "Do not be afraid, for I know that you are looking for Jesus, who was crucified. He is not here; he has risen, just as he said" (Matthew 28:5–6).

There is a world of difference between "he is no more" and "he is not here; he has risen."

I will be with Yeshu Baba, because he is Jesus, the Savior of the world.

Chapter 4

HONOR, SHAME, AND JESUS

Abdu Murray

"Then you will know that I am the LORD;
those who wait for me shall not be put to shame."

ISAIAH 49:23 ESV

The young Indian man's words echoed in my ears as he muttered them with his head bowed. "My father has never told me that he is proud of me," he said. "And if I become a Christian, he never will."

For a young person from the East, earning a parent's approval and delight rival every other aim in life. Several times during the course of our conversation, this young man said he'd already spent a lot of time looking at the evidence for Christianity and found it to be quite credible. Yet in an effort to forestall a decision he knew would bring shame to his family, he kept asking me questions he'd already found the answers to. He had intellectually assented to the gospel. He just couldn't bring himself to embrace the gospel.

To Western minds, such a predicament may seem like no predicament at all. *How can someone agree that a particular worldview is true but not believe in it?* one might ask. Indeed, for those awash in the West's love affair with individualism and personal choice, such a situation seems quite foreign. For the Easterner and Middle Easterner, whose cultures are collectivist and communal, the young Indian man's plight isn't so alien. For them, community and family honor underpin and dominate all of life's pursuits, even the pursuit of truth.[1]

That's why a thoughtful young man can intellectually assent to the truth of the gospel and yet be terrified at the very idea of embracing it as true. To his credit, he knew that if he embraced the gospel and became a Christian, he would eventually have to live out his faith. That was the problem, of course. *If he lost his family's approval, he would lose himself. If he lost himself, who would he be?*

I could relate to his fear of losing his identity. I too came from a non-Christian religious background, specifically Islam. I too feared that if I became a Christian, I would shame myself and everyone I loved. I too derived my identity through adherence to the religion of my birth. I too was once terrified of not knowing who I would be. The truth of the gospel and the answers it provides are not hard to find. Honor and shame, however, make them hard to accept.

This phenomenon happens with Westerners, of course, but perhaps not with the intensity Easterners and Middle Easterners may experience. Still, as we'll see, understanding the role of shame and honor isn't merely a journey of curiosity about a foreign culture for Westerners. Understanding it can teach them quite a bit about themselves as well. Fear of bringing shame to oneself is real in the West, but it has been comparatively uncommon, given the Western emphasis on individualism. Today, with the ever-rising tide of social media and society's ability to mass shame people for their opinions or beliefs, the West can afford to learn a few lessons from the East about how honor and shame affect our pursuit of truth.

Eastern cultures are collectivistic or communal, which means that each person's value, dignity, integrity, and very identity are derived from how he or she is perceived by the community. Perpetuating an Eastern community's traditions, especially its religious traditions, brings honor. Breaking from tradition, especially religious tradition, brings shame. In the East and Middle East, if perceived honor bestows identity on a person, perceived shame robs him of it. Understanding this can teach the West that there is a world of difference between intellectually assenting to a worldview as true and existentially embracing it as your own.

A better appreciation for the power of honor and shame can yield at least three important insights. First, we gain a clearer understanding of biblical stories and lessons that may otherwise be cloudy to Western eyes. Second, we confront the most powerful barriers Easterners face in considering whether the gospel may be true, and we learn how to scale those barriers. Third, we gain insight into how honor and shame affect all of us, both Eastern and Western, and how Jesus profoundly speaks to us all.

SEEING THE BIBLE'S BACKDROP

I have loved orchestral music since I was a teenager. My dear friend Mickey introduced me to some of my favorites. Mickey earned a degree in music composition alongside his computer engineering degree. When we would go to a Mozart concert together, I would *enjoy* it. But Mickey—with his understanding of music theory, theme development, modulations, and the like—would be *enraptured* by the composer's genius.

Depth of understanding can elevate one's experience from mere enjoyment to exultation. In the same way, deepening our understanding of how honor and shame serve as the Bible's cultural backdrop can illuminate its depths for all of us.

"There is more said in the Bible about shame and honor than about guilt and innocence," writes Simon Chan.[2] Intuitively, Chan's statement seems right. Though the Bible has much to say about guilt and innocence, perhaps its shame and honor undertones leap out to me more obviously because of my Middle Eastern heritage, a heritage that emphasizes shame and honor as potent social forces. The Bible, being a Middle Eastern book, would naturally speak to the cultural—and theological—impacts of honor and shame.

We often interpret our relationship with God through the familiar lenses of our relationships with each other. In the West, an important way we structure human relationships is through innocence and guilt. Someone who has wronged me (say, by lying, speaking ill of me, or stealing a promotion) feels guilty because of what he has done. In an innocence-guilt framework, feelings of guilt often plague our consciences—manifesting themselves as anxiety, distracted thinking, and even confession—regardless of whether we've been caught or how society may perceive us.

In non-Western honor-shame cultures, however, one's moral emphasis and enforcement are usually external. An Easterner may have done something wrong and yet feel no conscience-plaguing guilt until someone else finds out about it. While there may be an internal recognition of the misdeed and even bad feelings about it, such feelings may not rise to the level of repentance or confession until it becomes inevitable that the family or community will discover it. Whereas in innocence-guilt cultures, one's individual desire to be free of a guilty conscience may impel a person to do the right thing, in an honor-shame culture, fear of disappointing family and the community and shaming oneself are the primary motivators for behaviors and beliefs. Because what one believes may bring honor or shame, choosing what one believes can be just as immoral as choosing what one does.

It would be a mistake, however, to think that Westerners have a stronger internal sense of right and wrong than Easterners. The fact is that honor and shame can have catastrophic internal impacts for Easterners. In an honor-shame framework, once someone's misdeeds are made known, it defines who they are as a person. Juliet November succinctly summarizes the difference between innocence-guilt and honor-shame frameworks this way: In an innocence-guilt framework, I would *feel* guilty because I have "done something bad"; in an honor-shame framework, I'd *be* guilty because "I am bad" in society's eyes.[3]

November offers a helpful illustration. An administrator for a company's Asian office was questioned because it was unclear whether funds had improperly gone into her account from the American office. It was later discovered to be only an accounting error. So as far as the Americans were concerned, the matter was resolved. The Asian administrator still felt the shame, however, because her integrity had been called into question. When the Americans never apologized for questioning her publicly, she eventually quit.[4]

We must not gloss over this too quickly. Honor and shame are such powerful forces that they affect how an Easterner sees himself or herself, even if he or she has done nothing wrong. This is why an Easterner may feel soul-crushing shame for changing their religious allegiance from the family's traditions, even if the newfound faith is true. They've done nothing wrong—except drop a shame bomb into their family's living room.[5]

MORAL TRUTHS THAT TRANSCEND CULTURE

Given all of this, one could be tempted to think that the Bible—being written and transmitted primarily to and through an honor-shame culture—subscribes to a morality dictated by cultural norms rather than objective, transcendent truths. Even a casual reading of Scripture debunks such an idea.

King David was called a "man after his [God's] own heart" (1 Samuel 13:14; Acts 13:22), yet he committed a horrible act of adultery, followed by a murder to cover it up (see 2 Samuel 11:1–27). Through the cover-up, David dodged public shame, the culturally subjective method of moral enforcement. Yet the objective moral reality eventually caught up with the king. While society was unaware of his shameful acts, the Bible says that "the thing that David had done displeased the LORD" (2 Samuel 11:27 ESV). God revealed David's sins to Nathan the prophet and sent him to unveil the sin right before the king (see 2 Samuel 12:1–14).

The publicity of the sin, even though known to only one other person, produced enough shame to stir David's conscience to bitter repentance. Interestingly, David publicized his own shame and remorse by penning these words to God, the Being who grounds objective morality: "For I know my transgressions, and my sin is ever before me. *Against you, you only*, have I sinned and done what is evil *in your sight*" (Psalm 51:3–4 ESV, emphasis mine).[6] God had used the scaffolding of an honor-shame framework to cage David's conscience.

This is why the Bible richly speaks to both honor-shame and innocence-guilt cultures. Its stories speak to Eastern minds by paying more than mere lip service to the power of communal honor and shame. It appeals to the Western mind by addressing the inner conscience that helps us see objective right and wrong.

SHAME IS THE NAME OF THE GAME

Even in the days before I became a Christian, I was struck by the dynamics of Jesus' social interactions. People questioned him with one of two different motives—either a sincere desire to understand his teachings or a desire to publicly discredit him. Recognizing the honor-shame backdrop of Jesus' Eastern culture elucidates what was happening in biblical scenes of people questioning Jesus and why Jesus responded as he did.

Consider Jesus' (many) confrontations with religious leaders who were so preoccupied with appearances and following religious rules that they invented rules of their own so that the people could see how pious they were. They were often at odds with Jesus, because he challenged their invented traditions and their desire to be noticed by others for their religiosity. Yet not all the religious leaders who questioned Jesus intended to shame him. Some came to him wanting to know the truth. Whether there was an audience during their questioning is the first clue about their intent.

When someone questioned Jesus privately, it was usually for the purpose of truly learning. For example, Nicodemus, a Pharisee and a member of the ruling council, came to Jesus under cover of night wanting to know who Jesus was and what his teaching meant (John 3:1–21). On the other hand, when Jesus was questioned with crowds nearby, it is a good bet that his questioners hoped to publicly shame him. E. Randolph Richards and Brandon O'Brien explain how these public questionings functioned as a part of what scholars call an honor game: "Public questions were contests. The winner was determined by the audience, who represented the community. If you silenced your opponent, you gained honor and they lost some."[7]

This dynamic clarifies a few puzzling phrases in the New Testament. Matthew records that after two public challenges—one with the politically minded Herodians, another with the pietistic Sadducees—Jesus' challengers were silenced; the crowds were amazed and astonished; and no one dared "to ask him any more questions" (Matthew 22:46 ESV). The Herodians tried to trap Jesus with a catch-22 political question of loyalty to Rome, intending to cost him his public honor with the people who despised their Roman occupiers or get him executed by those same occupiers for insurrection. The Sadducees tried to make Jesus' teachings on the resurrection look absurd by asking him who a woman would be married to in the afterlife if she remarried after her first husband died.

In both cases, Jesus played the honor game like a master, flipping the attempts to publicly shame him onto his challengers, while giving honor to those in the crowds who needed to hear his message. The Herodians and Sadducees had played the honor game and lost. They couldn't risk losing any more honor before the crowds, which explains why they didn't dare ask him any more public questions. The crowds understood what Jesus had done and how he had honored their dignity in the process, which explains why they were astonished and amazed.

SHAME LEADING TO FEAR— FEAR GIVING WAY TO HONOR

Why is it so important to understand the role honor and shame played in how people asked questions two thousand years ago in the Middle East? Partly to better understand biblical accounts about Jesus, but also because not much has changed in twenty centuries of human interaction around the world. Honor-shame insights can help us see whether a pursuit of truth is at the heart of our exchanges with others and whether we ourselves are interested in truth or in winning rhetorical games.

A series of questions I fielded at a recent church open forum comes to mind. Attendees had the option of asking their questions at microphones or anonymously through text messages. What stood out was the disparity of tone between questions asked by those at microphones and those asked by text messages, especially among the Easterners. Several Muslims came up to the microphones and asked important but blunt questions like, "Where in the Bible does Jesus say, 'I'm God; worship me'?" and "How could God be just if he makes the innocent Jesus pay for my sins by dying on the cross?" One Muslim even asked, "Why would God send a son and not a daughter? In Christianity, if God is Father, why not send a daughter to be fair?" (I wasn't sure how serious that last question was, but I answered it anyway.) The point is that the questions posed in front of the crowd were blunt and challenging. But another question that came from a Muslim by text message stood out for its contrastingly introspective tone. "I'm a Muslim, and I believe in the existence of God. But still I feel bored and meaningless. Why is that?"

My answer wasn't nearly as interesting as the question itself. In an honor-shame culture, the Muslim questioner likely wouldn't dare expose such doubts openly. Technology's anonymity allowed the question to be asked (thank God) and answered. The fact that such a question could be posed because it wasn't attached to a name or a face tells us a lot about the sway honor and shame hold over Easterners.

They were powerful in Jesus' day, and they remain just as powerful today.

Jesus appreciated the Eastern desire to preserve honor but emphasized that true honor is bestowed by God, not human beings. He explained that those who suffer for following him will be blessed because "the Father will *honor* him" (John 12:26 ESV, emphasis mine).

Among those who heard him were religious authorities who actually believed in him, unlike others among their ranks who regularly challenged Jesus. Yet they feared publicizing their beliefs "so that they would not be put out of the synagogue; for they loved the glory that comes from man more than the glory that comes from God" (John 12:42–43 ESV). Isn't it fascinating that the desire for public honor and the dread of communal shame loom so ominously that they can eclipse even the very truth we've come to believe?

Let's return to the story in John 9 that Ravi referred to in chapter 3. There we read that Jesus encountered a young man who had to resort to the culturally shameful act of begging because he had been born blind. The flint that ignited a confrontation between Jesus and the Pharisees was that Jesus healed the young man's sight by making mud and putting it on his eyelids, thereby performing "work" on the Sabbath day of rest. The Pharisees initially thought that a ruse was afoot—perhaps the supposedly healed man was a scammer who only resembled the person the town knew to have been blind. So they asked his parents if he was really their son and, if so, how it was that he could now see: "We know that this is our son and that he was born blind," they responded. "But how he now sees we do not know, nor do we know who opened his eyes" (verses 20–21 ESV). Referring to their newly sighted son, they said, "Ask him; he is of age. He will speak for himself."

Allow me to speculate a bit. The parents' statement that "he is of age" implies that their son mustn't have looked all that grown-up, perhaps being barely older than the Jewish age of adulthood. Yet his parents were so afraid to answer the Pharisees' questions forthrightly that they threw their young son to the wolves: "His parents said these things because they feared the Jews, for the Jews had already agreed that if anyone should confess Jesus to be Christ, he was to be put out of the synagogue" (verse 22 ESV). Being put out of the synagogue would have been the biggest public shame of all.

Hover over the parents for a moment longer. Their son was freed from the lifelong ignominy of having to beg. They received the miracle they likely had prayed for for years but wouldn't publicly acknowledge the one who performed it. To avoid their own shame, they dishonored God.

Their son's response stands in stark contrast. The way the Pharisees opened their round of interrogation of him is just shy of hilarious. "Give glory [i.e., honor] to God," they ordered him in ironic hypocrisy. "We know that this man [Jesus] is a sinner . . . What did he do to you? How did he open your eyes?" (verses 24, 26 ESV).

The young man's sarcasm highlights his lack of intimidation. "I have told you already, and you would not listen. Why do you want to hear it again?" he asked. "Do you also want to become his disciples?" (verse 27 ESV).

Incensed that a lowly beggar would publicly challenge their authority, the Pharisees barked back, "You were born in utter sin, and would you teach us?" (verse 34 ESV). Unable to handle the public challenge, they delivered the communal shame knockout punch by casting the man out of the synagogue.

Jesus' radar for unjustified shaming drove him to seek the young man out. With tender authority, Jesus revealed that he is the promised Messiah. He gave the young man not only the honor of physical sight but also the higher honor of spiritual sight. "For judgment I came into this world," says Jesus, "that those who do not see may see, and those who see may become blind" (verse 39 ESV). Jesus simply would not let the Pharisees rob the young man of the honor he had been given by casting him out of the synagogue. Jesus replaced a temporary social honor bestowed by hypocrites with the transcendent honor bestowed only by God.

BARRIERS BUILT WITH SHAME-SHAPED BRICKS

As I mentioned earlier, in the West, with such a strong focus on individualism and freedom of choice, changing one's religious views generally hasn't been seen as morally positive or negative. Indeed, generally it's considered morally wrong for the collective to impose its will on an individual's conscience or choices. In the East, however, the opposite is usually the case. Eastern collectivism dictates that morality is about what's good for the community and family first. What's good for the individual comes second. Upholding tradition is considered best for the community and family. Thus, changing one's religious affiliation is a moral choice—an *immoral* choice in the eyes of most.

Eastern families fiercely care for their children, but buoyed by hopes of how their children might enhance family honor, they also put them on unreasonably high pedestals. I recently met an intelligent and accomplished Muslim from Pakistan. With an ease of the tongue and a strong vocabulary, he described his exploration of Christianity and how reasonable he was finding it to be. "It just makes sense. So many of the important issues of life and society are answered well by Christianity. Islam, on the other hand, seems to offer very little."

I was intrigued as to where this might be heading. "If you agree with all of that, is there anything holding you back from putting your faith in Jesus fully and publicly?" I knew the answer to that question, of course.

His eyes found something on the floor that allowed him to avoid looking at me as he spoke. "Well, my family, I suppose," he muttered. "I'd be terrified of losing them. My father would never accept this, even with all the education and open-mindedness he has instilled in me." It was a long way of saying, *I can't become a Christian because the pedestal I've been put atop is too high to fall from.*

When a Muslim, a Hindu, or a Buddhist becomes a Christian, her family and community feel that she has elevated her individualism above the community and family. She has betrayed everyone, especially family, by what is seen as a selfish act. Her choice is denounced; she is shunned; and her parents are scorned for having failed to instill proper values in their child.

A friend's story illustrates the paradoxical push-pull of communal honor and filial love. This friend was raised as a Muslim in Iraq and converted to Christianity as a young adult. His brothers, furious, threatened to kill him. Fearing they would make good on the threats, his mother arranged to get him out of the country. As she dropped him off at the airport, she gave him tear-filled kisses on his cheeks.

Then she spat in his face and said, "Now you're dead to me."

He never saw her again. In an honor-shame framework, exercising the right to choose one's religion by following the evidence wherever it may lead isn't about *doing* something bad (incurring guilt); it's about *becoming* someone bad.

Shame's effect is not just external either. The Easterner who considers converting to Christianity from another faith stands at the edge of an internal precipice. A change in self-identity is at stake. A Hindu who professes faith in Christ doesn't merely stop being a Hindu. She also falls from the pedestal of being her family's pride and joy, landing in the ditch of being the family's dirty little secret. Easterners know all too well this fear of plummeting from the edge of identity's cliff, not knowing who they'll be if they embrace the gospel. With that kind of pressure, is it any wonder that Easterners, whether Muslim, Hindu, Buddhist, or otherwise, can be so resistant to the gospel, even when its truth is powerfully presented, even when it is assented to?

SAVED IN TRANSLATION

The poetic irony is that while honor and shame can erect barriers to the gospel, they can also pave boulevards to Christian belief. Westerners tend to understand and present the gospel in terms of innocence and guilt: we were created innocent, as creatures made in God's image, to have communion with him. But starting with Adam and Eve and ending with ourselves, we have transgressed God's law and stand guilty before him. To deal with blameworthiness, Christ—who is not only innocent but sinless in his nature as both God and man—acts as our representative, just as Adam and Eve were our representatives. Our guilt is fastened onto Jesus at the cross. God the Son pays the penalty for us to God the Father. Thus justice is served; mercy is bestowed; and we stand innocent. That is an accurate summary of the gospel.

But honor and shame frame an equally accurate summary of the gospel. We had the honor of being in God's presence but experienced the shame of what it means to reject him (Genesis 3:7–11). Jesus came to restore us to honor by bearing our shame (Psalm 22; Isaiah 53:3–4, 8–9; Matthew 27:46; Mark 15:34). That is why theologians often refer to Jesus' incarnation as his "state of humiliation." He humbled himself and took on the form of a servant, letting go of his status as divine master and taking human form (Philippians 2:6–8). As he was restored to glory and honor by his resurrection, we too are restored to the honor of fellowship with God (Romans 5:6–11; Philippians 2:9–11).

As we can see, the Bible is multilingual. Its message translates well between honor-shame and innocence-guilt frameworks.

It may take a bit of effort to get the translation right though. The Eastern focus on honor and shame explains why some reject parts of the Bible not only as untrue but also as shamefully scandalous. The biblical narrative includes accounts of its most influential figures—from Adam and Eve to Noah, from Abraham and Sarah to King David and Solomon—as morally complex figures. They not only make *bad* decisions, but they make *immoral* ones that lead to marital infidelities, broken promises, and even murder.

I can recall sitting with an imam who told me that the Bible's unblushing descriptions of the prophets' shameful acts is one of the things that disqualify it as having come from God. In his view, prophets like those depicted in the Bible couldn't possibly be trusted to carry God's message to the people. The biblical prophets were, according to his reasoning, no more virtuous than those they were trying to reach. By comparison, the Qur'an and the Hadith, the chief Muslim holy sources, depict the prophets as paragons of virtue who always carried out the divine will without question or misstep.

Yet this statement allowed me to pave a boulevard to the credibility of the gospel with the imam. During law school, as I began to understand philosophies of evidence and how witness statements work, I began to walk down a similar boulevard as I saw how the very fact that the Bible describes its chief figures as sinful actually strengthens the case for its credibility. In courts around the world, hearsay is generally excluded from the evidence presented to the jury. While it's commonly misunderstood, hearsay is simply an out-of-court statement made by someone other than the witness who is reporting it.[8]

An example may help. Suppose a man named Tom is being sued, accused of starting a forest fire when the flame from a rifle he fired ignited extremely dry brush. A witness wants to testify that he heard another man named Roy say to the arriving firefighters that the usual "No Shooting: Dry Brush" sign was not up when Tom shot his rifle. That witness's testimony would be inadmissible hearsay at Tom's trial because Roy had made the statement about the sign outside of the jury's presence. Courts generally exclude testimony about such hearsay because the person who originally said it can't be cross-examined to test if the statement is true, biased, or based on faulty memory.

The hearsay rule has exceptions, however. I fondly recall my evidence professor in law school saying that the rule is sometimes "more hole than cheese." Those exceptions allow certain types of otherwise excludable hearsay because the surrounding circumstances lend credibility to the statement. If the witness in the example above testified that Roy said, "The usual 'No Shooting: Dry Brush' sign wasn't up when Tom shot his rifle *because I forgot to put the sign up that day*," then the witness's testimony could be admitted under the exception that allows the jury to consider hearsay testimony when it's a statement made against the interest of the person saying it.[9] The rationale is that Roy's out-of-court statement made Roy look bad (and even responsible for the fire), which means that he likely wouldn't have made that statement if it weren't true. In other words, Roy's embarrassing admission that he forgot to put up the sign gives the rest of his statement more credibility, not less. Ironically, "shameful" facts can lead us toward truth, not away from it.

There's something similar in the study of history called "the principle of embarrassment." According to this principle, a historical account is more likely to be true if it includes embarrassing or damaging details about the heroic figures or the person giving the account. When legends pop up about historical figures, the hero tends to become more heroic, not less. George Washington chops down cherry trees and confesses his mistake to his father because he cannot tell a lie. Robin Hood goes from a swashbuckling thief to someone who not only stole from the rich to give to the poor but also opposed evil authorities who tried to take the place of the rightful king.

The Bible contains stories that don't look anything like such legends. God chooses Noah to carry on the human race after judgment came, but later Noah gets embarrassingly drunk (Genesis 9:21–22). God miraculously fulfills his promise to Abraham that he'd have a son and that he'd be the father of many nations. Yet Abraham tells half-truths about his wife's identity to save his own skin (Genesis 12:10–20; 20:1–13). David is called a man after God's own heart, yet he not only commits adultery; he also murders the husband to cover it up. God grants Solomon's request to be made wise (1 Kings 3–4) and sanctions Solomon as the builder of the temple (1 Kings 5–6), yet Solomon gives in to his base desires, leading to his eventual destruction (1 Kings 11). Jesus' disciples are often depicted as hotheaded, self-centered, and a bit dim. On one occasion, Jesus even calls Peter "Satan" for failing to understand God's redemptive plan (Matthew 16:23).

All of these are embarrassing, even downright shameful, details about biblical figures. When we consider the fact that Jesus' disciples actually wrote some of those details about themselves, they are not only embarrassing; they are declarations against interest. Like hearsay statements that gain credibility by including shameful details, the Bible's accounts gain credibility because they depict how God has moved in human history and used real, quite flawed people for his work. In other words, the Bible would have no reason to include such shameful details unless it is telling us how things really happened.

Muslims often shun the idea of Jesus dying on a cross because it is so shameful. Similarly, the Hindu philosopher Radhakrishnan remarked that "a suffering God, a deity with a crown of thorns, cannot satisfy the religious soul."[10] To stress Jesus' honorific status, the Qur'an denies the historical reality that he was crucified to death on a cross (see Qur'an 4:157–158). Such shameful treatment, the thinking goes, would have discredited Jesus in the people's eyes, which is why God kept Jesus from it. Fear of shame explains the various Islamic accounts for what happened to Jesus. The Qur'an enigmatically claims that "they killed him not, nor crucified him, but so it was made to appear to them" (Qur'an 4:157) and offers no other explanation of what *did* "appear to them." Muslim commentators suggest it wasn't Jesus on the cross, but a substitute for Jesus, perhaps Simon of Cyrene, Judas Iscariot, or even a volunteer from among Jesus' followers.[11]

But do these theories really protect Jesus from shame? Is it true that a suffering God cannot satisfy the religious soul? Don't the Islamic theories, especially the theory that Jesus allowed one of his followers to be painfully killed in his place, sound more like shameful cowardice? That Jesus actually suffered willingly and defeated death by rising from the grave sounds more like courage, honor, and glory.

Muslims and Hindus—being Eastern—appreciate the depths of shame, which is why they fervently downplay (or outright deny) Jesus' crucifixion. I can certainly relate. I would rather suffer the stabs of a thousand needles than see tears fall from a parent's eyes, especially if they were shed out of shame. The very fact that the Easterner appreciates shame's profundity allows us to communicate the magnitude of what Jesus accomplished at the cross. Jesus anticipated the joy of fulfilling God the Father's will that we should be saved from our shame and guilt. The paradox is that in bearing our shame for us, Jesus performed an honorable act. Jesus took shame's momentum, flipped it around, and turned it into honor. It is he "who for the joy that was set before him endured the cross, despising the shame, and is seated at the right hand of the throne of God" (Hebrews 12:2 ESV). Someone who slinks away from suffering cannot give us honor. Someone who takes on our shame and rises above it is the only one who can satisfy the Eastern soul.

A PASSPORT WITH MANY STAMPS

Appreciating honor and shame as social and moral influences can communicate truth as much to Westerners as it can to Easterners. The Bible drips with insights into how all of us— Eastern or Western, innocence-seeking or honor-loving— respond to truth. One can easily misunderstand and infer that the differences between honor-shame cultures and innocence-guilt cultures draw sharp distinctions between the two. The overlap, in fact, is significant. Easterners may stress public honor and shame as means to promote private virtue (innocence) and prevent personal guilt (wrongdoing). Westerners tend to reverse the emphasis. If someone obeys their personally felt ethics and does what is right, that person receives public honor. If the person flouts her conscience, she may feel private shame. Honor-shame cultures differ from innocence-guilt cultures only in terms of *emphasis*, not substance.

I recently read the heartbreaking story of Anne Darwin, whose deceit landed her not only in legal trouble but also in a pit of public shame. Her husband, John Darwin, had concocted a plan to collect life insurance proceeds by having Anne claim he was lost at sea during a canoe trip. After five years of Anne trying to perpetuate the lie, their ruse was finally exposed as she and her husband were spotted living together in Panama. Their hoax cost multiple thousands of dollars as authorities searched for John.

Anne Darwin was found guilty of fraud and served time in prison. She was called "fraudster, consummate liar, wicked, and selfish," but the label that wounded her the most wasn't about legal guilt. The moniker that cut her deepest was *bad mother.*

Her loving sons had sustained their belief in her for the five-year marathon of lies, only to have their hearts seize in their chests as the truth of what their mother did became undeniable. For her sons, "the betrayal was so sustained, and so humiliating, they publicly said they never wanted to see their mother again." Although Anne and her boys are reconciled at long last, the scars and shame remained.[12] Yes, in this story involving Westerners, there was legal and personal guilt. Yet the seemingly unwashable stain was the shame.

Who can forget the Clinton–Lewinsky scandal of the 1990s? Then–President Bill Clinton engaged in an extramarital affair with a young intern, only to deny it by saying, "I did not have sexual relations with that woman, Ms. Lewinsky." Quickly, it came to light that both had breached private and public trusts. Guilt bled through the veil of innocence. What fascinated me, however, was a speech I watched Monica Lewinsky deliver years later. It wasn't her guilt that persisted and almost drove her to suicide. It was the public shame, delivered Western style. "There are no perimeters around how many people can publicly observe you and put you in a public stockade," she said, describing the age of social media. "This shift," she continued, "has created what Professor Nicolaus Mills calls a culture of humiliation."[13] It was painful to hear Ms. Lewinsky list off the names she was called so publicly and repeatedly. "I was branded as a tramp, tart, slut, whore, bimbo, and, of course, *that woman*. I was seen by many but actually known by few. And I get it. It was easy to forget that *that woman* was dimensional, had a soul, and was once unbroken."[14]

Perhaps I read more into her expression than was warranted, but I couldn't help but see the pain behind her eyes at being labeled *that woman* so dismissively by the other guilty party. Perhaps that label was a way to shame her into silence, to marginalize her voice. Who knows?

What Anne Darwin's and Monica Lewinsky's stories show is that Easterners have not cornered the market on the honor and shame game. The vitriol and name-calling across all media today stem from the devaluing of other people (what I call the "Hitlerization of social commentary" in my book

Saving Truth) and have resulted in the culture of humiliation that Monica Lewinsky laments and almost lost her life to. I suspect that Westerners can relate—perhaps all too well— with Eastern sensibilities of honor and shame. Indeed, the honor-shame framework has a passport with many stamps.

WHERE SHAME AND GUILT MEET INNOCENCE AND HONOR

The cross draws together so many aspects of life, history, and existence itself. That may read like an overblown claim, grandiose to the point of being ridiculous—but I'm convinced it's not, especially when it comes to honor, shame, guilt, and innocence. Our guilt that causes shame was borne by the innocent Jesus, who thereby restored our honor. Guilt and honor, innocence and shame, all dance through the ages and the pages of Scripture, culminating in the cross.

The same King David who committed adultery and murder looked forward to the way in which God would redeem him and his people from both their guilt and their shame. "O my God, in you I trust," he writes. "Let me not be put to shame; let not my enemies exult over me. Indeed, none who wait for you shall be put to shame" (Psalm 25:2–3 ESV). Just a few verses later, David couples forgiveness of guilt with the preservation of honor: "For your name's sake, O LORD, pardon my guilt, for it is great" (Psalm 25:11 ESV). God pardons *our* guilt, which brings honor to *his* name. As our innocence is restored and God is honored, moral integrity preserves us so that we can avoid both guilt and shame.

"May integrity and uprightness preserve me, for I wait for you," David prays (Psalm 25:21 ESV). Guilt absolved leads to honor restored.

Calvary's hill is where the dance between all of these facets of life ends with a grace-empowered lift, thereby speaking to both Eastern and Western hearts. Much like the guilty criminal who owes a debt to society, each of us in our guilt of sin owes a debt to God. But it is a debt we can never hope to pay without utter separation from God. Jesus went to the cross for us, to pay the debt we owe, because he has no debts of his own to pay.

The gospel of John conveys with the Greek word *tetelestai* Jesus' dying declaration that his crucifixion had accomplished his earthly mission. It is a financial term roughly meaning "paid in full," and it is wholly appropriate to describe what happened because Jesus paid our debt of guilt. The cross was more than just transactional, however. It was a humiliating way to be executed. Jesus was stripped and splayed out just outside the gates of Jerusalem, the Holy City. Thus did Jesus fulfill the Mosaic law's requirement for two kinds of sacrifices—a spotless animal to bear the people's shame and be sent out of the community and a spotless animal that would bear the people's guilt and be slain. He was both flung outside the gates of the community, carrying away our shame, and killed in our place, paying our debt to God.[15]

As honor and shame (mostly shame) gain prevalence in the West, restitution is becoming increasingly inadequate to remedy a guilt-worthy act. Something more needs to be done for the stains to be lifted. "Removing the shame is a more complex process than just paying the penalty for guilt because it involves a restoration of the shamed person's image of themselves, as well as a restoration of their status, within their community," Juliet November tells us.[16]

This is why the gospel's remedy can translate to both East and West so well. The Greek word *Telos*—which means "purpose"—is the root of the word *tetelestai*, which conveyed Jesus' declaration that his death fully paid our debts. In other words, Jesus' sacrifice had the purpose of restoring us to our original image and status as those who were honored and innocent before God.

Anne Darwin's story of shame and forgiveness is as much Eastern as it is Western. Legally, she will ever bear the guilt-laden moniker "convicted felon." But she has reconciled with her sons. The shame-charred brand "bad mother" is fading from her. Our reconciliation to the Creator of the universe through Jesus fades our branded scars as well. He restores for each of us the beautiful image originally given us by God.

The hymn writer Isaac Watts captures the depth and beauty of this so well:

> *The Lord is just and kind,*
> *The meek shall learn his ways,*
> *And every humble sinner find*
> *The methods of his grace.*

> *For his own goodness' sake*
> *He saves my soul from shame:*
> *He pardons, though my guilt be great,*
> *Through my Redeemer's name.*[17]

Through Christ, God casts our shame across an impassable distance: "As far as the east is from the west, so far does he remove our transgressions from us" (Psalm 103:12 ESV). The young Indian man I met with at the beginning of this chapter has since given his life to Jesus and has found the honor for which he was searching. So many born in the West have overcome shame by embracing the gospel. East and West may be a world apart geographically, but in their shared need for restored honor and innocence, at the cross they can meet spiritually and be satisfied.

Chapter 5

THE REWARDS
OF SACRIFICE

Abdu Murray

For I am not ashamed of the gospel, for it is the
power of God for salvation to everyone who
believes, to the Jew first and also to the Greek.

ROMANS 1:16 ESV

Like so many New Testament passages, the potency (but not meaning) of Romans 1:16 varies, depending on the social context in which one reads it. In the West, it's becoming increasingly uncomfortable to share traditional Christian convictions, especially as they collide with prevailing cultural opinions on issues like sexuality, race, gender, and even economics. In the 1980s and 1990s, there was very little stigma attached to the labels "Christian" or "evangelical." In those days, Paul's call to boldness may only have had a bumper sticker impact, inspiring the comfortably faithful to say "amen," probably because they didn't have to worry about being publicly or digitally shamed for holding Christian convictions. Comfortable contexts cause comfortable eyes to breeze past verses like Romans 1:16.

But in recent years, things have shifted. With social media movements like "#exposechristianschools" trending and strident calls for Christian institutions to be investigated for hate speech, Romans 1:16 squeezes our hearts more. Paul's words elicit hard questions within. *Am I really unashamed of the gospel? Do I really believe it is the power of salvation for everyone? Am I willing to lose relationships or even my carefully planned future for its message?*

A pause is necessary here. Christians are increasingly criticized for having a persecution complex while being among the safest people in the West. Some argue that Christianity has never really suffered an age of persecution, maybe not even in its infancy under Roman rule.

It's true that the term *persecution* can be (and has been) loosely thrown around. To some, it means getting teased for being a Christian. For others, it means being killed for being a Christian. It is categorically false, however, to claim that Christians have not suffered persecution or that they don't live under persecution's shadow today. In China, the government tolerates existing churches but occasionally cracks down on them, forcibly shutting their doors if they prove too successful. In the Middle East and Africa, we need only look at the past few years' headlines to see that persecution of Christians happens with ghoulish ferocity. According to a study commissioned by the British foreign secretary, in the Middle East, Africa, and Asia, "the level and nature of persecution is arguably coming close to meeting the international definition of genocide."[1]

Compared to the axes and whips Christians in the East and Africa face, Western Christians may suffer metaphorical slaps across the cheek, perhaps the occasional right cross to the jaw. But Western anti-Christian sentiment is increasing. This is why it is crucial for Western Christians to learn how Eastern and Middle Eastern Christians have (and are) enduring pain because of their faith. In fact, they aren't just enduring it; they are flourishing because of it. In the East and Middle East, being unashamed of the gospel means more than just risking invites to parties, losing job promotions, or not getting into a favorite university. It could mean loss of freedom and even loss of life. But it also means gaining blessings that are not otherwise attainable.

I am about to touch on a story that seems to contradict that last statement. If you'll allow me to develop the idea, however, you'll see that it actually serves to prove it.

TWENTY-ONE MEN

In 2015, the terrorist group ISIS published a gruesome video in which their operatives viciously murdered twenty-one Coptic Christians. The imagery of what transpired on the Mediterranean shore has now burned itself into our collective consciousness. The twenty-one Christians were all young men from Egypt. They were draped in bright orange jumpsuits, much like prison uniforms. Behind each of them stood an executioner shrouded in jet black, face covered. The Christians were not blindfolded. Their faces, unlike those of the cowards who took their lives, were on display for all to see. They were forced to their knees, facing away from their captors. They had been told that if they renounced their faith in Christ, their lives would be spared. None of those men took the offer. As the blades touched their necks, the victims shouted or mouthed the words *Ya Rab Yesua!* (Oh, Lord Jesus!). They called out to the Light of the world as cowardly men robed in darkness brutalized them.

As kids, those twenty-one men likely played in dusty Middle Eastern streets with the carefree attitude that only children can display—even if only momentarily—amid the tragedies their homeland has endured. How far away those playful moments must have felt as they were faced with a terrible ultimatum. Did memories of those days rush through their heads? Did the faint aromas of bread baking in their mothers' welcoming kitchens transport their minds away from the terrible scene they found themselves in? Did they worry about how much it would hurt before they would meet their heavenly Father? Did they scan the Mediterranean's horizon, searching for some angelic host or armed troupe to save them from such terror? Where is the supposed blessing in such a situation? How can someone like me, sitting in a comfortable chair in the United States, so cavalierly claim that blessing emerges from such horror?

I have experienced my share of suffering just for becoming a Christian. I've also received immeasurable and innumerable blessings just for the fact of being a Christian. In fact, I would say I have often felt most blessed when it's been difficult to profess my faith in Jesus. During his all too short life, my dear friend Nabeel Qureshi experienced similar pain and would agree that blessed closeness to God coincides with pain for following him. Perhaps this gives me and Nabeel some credibility on the topic of blessing from pain. Yet neither Nabeel nor I have experienced anything close to what those twenty-one men suffered. They are the very definition of credibility on the subject, as we'll soon see. Their resilient faith punctuates the words "for I am not ashamed of the gospel" with twenty-one exclamation points.

While their steadfastness in the face of death is inspiring, it's also discomfiting. They have forced us to ask if we would have that kind of courage and integrity. The question that naturally arises is this: *What could have made such men so brave? What could have been so wonderful that they were willing to trade their lives for it?* Let me say this from experience and on the authority of history, on the authority of what those twenty-one men withstood, and on the authority of Scripture: blessing doesn't incidentally arise out of suffering for one's faith; specific blessings are bestowed because of that suffering.

THE INEVITABILITY OF SUFFERING FOR FAITH

Indeed, all who desire to live a godly life in Christ Jesus will be persecuted.

2 TIMOTHY 3:12 ESV

"A servant is not greater than his master," Jesus told his disciples. "If they persecuted me, they will also persecute you" (John 15:20 ESV). Following Jesus means living as he lived. Sometimes it means being loved as one who sacrificially helps people. Other times it means being reviled as someone who challenges people. In many parts of the world, it also means dying as he died.

Knowing that people would be offended by his message that sinful humanity needs a Savior, Jesus directly told his disciples (and indirectly tells us) that "they *will* lay their hands on you and persecute you, delivering you up to the synagogues and prisons, and you will be brought before kings and governors for my name's sake" (Luke 21:12 ESV, emphasis mine). Jesus didn't say it may happen; he said it *will* happen. Now, it's important to note that Jesus was speaking to his disciples as a group and in a pre-Christian context. When he told them "they will persecute *you*" and "they will lay their hands on *you*," the "yous" are plural, equivalent to saying "you guys" or "y'all." Jesus is saying that Christians in general will suffer persecution, even if suffering for the faith is absent in an individual Christian's life. Today Jesus speaks to us corporately as well, not in a pre-Christian era, but in one that is decidedly post-Christian.

In the earliest years of the fledgling church, Paul (Saul as he was known then) had been one of the people to lay his hands on Christians and deliver them up to the authorities for preaching that Jesus was the Messiah. Jesus broke into Paul's world even as he was in the midst of persecuting Christians, transforming Paul from persecutor to persecuted (Acts 9). Thereafter, Paul spent his life proclaiming the message he once sought to silence. After suffering so much hardship, Paul wrote a touching letter to his young protégé Timothy. Paul encouraged Timothy in his faith but also told him this hard truth: "Indeed, all who desire to live a godly life in Christ Jesus will be persecuted" (2 Timothy 3:12 ESV).

Paul passed on to Timothy the same lesson with which Jesus had birthed Paul's ministry. Paul had been suddenly but temporarily blinded after first seeing the resurrected Jesus. A man named Judas took care of Paul at his home in Damascus. Still, Paul's reputation as a staunch persecutor had reached the ears of a Christian named Ananias. Jesus broke into Ananias's world too, directing him to visit Paul and inform him of his divine calling to preach the very gospel he once oppressed. Ananias hesitated to obey, fearing Paul's ferocity. But Jesus insisted. "Go," he said, "for he is a chosen instrument of mine to carry my name before the Gentiles and kings and the children of Israel." Then comes a curious statement: *"For I will show him how much he must suffer for the sake of my name"* (Acts 9:15–16 ESV, emphasis mine).

Christ will show Paul how much he must suffer? What a strange way for Jesus to invite Paul to preach his gospel. It's hardly an enticing invitation. Yet Paul's Eastern mind understood that suffering is intertwined with significance. When Paul accepted the calling, his sight was restored. Paul began to see what it meant to follow the One who saves the world by suffering for it.

That story challenges us so personally, doesn't it? When I first became a Christian, I kept it a close secret, telling only a few friends and the church community I had become part of. I wanted to avoid the pain of hurting or shaming those I loved. At first, keeping my faith under wraps seemed like the easy path. I was wrong.

Over the months, the joy-fueled flame of knowing I had

eternal life in Christ was dimming. My beliefs were becoming a pool of anxiety instead of a spring of joy. A friend noticed and told me with jarring sincerity that my secrecy was robbing me of joy. He quoted Jesus' words about Paul in Acts 9:16 to point out that pain is part and parcel of some people's faith walk. I knew in that moment that my fulfillment was tied to pain as well. I faced up to that pain, strengthened by Christ to do so.

My dear friend Nabeel, whom I miss terribly since his early death, had to face up to that pain when he told his loving parents he had become a Christian. Yet even as Nabeel's earthly life ebbed, he maintained his witness to his family. The family tensions continued, but his joy and steadfastness were all the more evident.

Currently there is a strong temptation to play the victimhood game, the winner of which is the one whose tribe has suffered the most injustice. Some groups have a legitimate—and quite unwanted—claim to victim status. Others manipulate the status to garner sympathy and support for an agenda. I will try my best here to avoid playing that grisly game of one-upmanship because the real losers are often those whose real plights get drowned out in the cacophony.

Of course, it isn't just Christians who suffer persecution. I recall a dinner conversation with a friend who is a highly placed executive within an organization dedicated to helping persecuted Christians. He told me that his organization collects data on persecution of many groups, not just Christians. Sadly, he told me, there are more instances than we might think of people bearing the label "Christian" who have persecuted other groups as well. Christians in the East and Middle

East are being persecuted, but so are other groups. Muslims persecute Christians in the Middle East, yet Muslims are persecuted by Buddhists in Southeast Asia. Ancient Buddhist statues are destroyed in Afghanistan. Atheists have been jailed or killed in the streets of some countries merely for making their worldview public. Suspected homosexuals have been thrown blindfolded from the tops of buildings.

In the Christian faith, however, suffering persecution is not incidental; it is inevitable. This doesn't mean that all Christians experience persecution. It means that some level of pain because of faith will come to every body of believers eventually.

I often wonder whether Western Christians have yet to feel an acute discomfort because they have failed to see pain's spiritually formative power. The time of ease appears to be coming to an end as Western values—which once found their footing in the Christian worldview—diverge from their roots. A friend who generously gives his time and treasure to humanitarian causes confided that he's bothered by the fact that he's never suffered for his faith. His comfort nags at him, suggesting that his lack of hardship has caused him to miss something important. His faith's genuineness doesn't depend on how much he's suffered, of course. Only half joking, I assured him that as social attitudes toward Christianity shift, he'll have plenty of opportunities to experience a little pain due to his convictions. Just as inevitable as the pain that comes from faith are the blessings that emerge from that pain. In fact, pain for the gospel's sake is more than inevitable. The Bible actually describes it as a gift.

We don't all have to have Paul's experiences of beatings

and execution to know what it means to be a Christian. I will say, however, that we have to be *willing* to have experiences like Paul's. Nabeel was willing. I remain willing. So many around the world have demonstrated their willingness to live like that. Why? Not because any one of us is braver than the next person, but because each of us has discovered that suffering for Christ isn't the only thing that is inevitable; so are his blessings. When we see that, we won't just be willing to experience pain; we may be eager to.

THE INEVITABILITY OF BLESSING

"No one who has left home or brothers or sisters or mother or father or children or fields for me and the gospel will fail to receive a hundred times as much in this present age: homes, brothers, sisters, mothers, children and fields—along with persecutions—and in the age to come eternal life."

JESUS, MARK 10:29-30

Looking forward to the blessing of being told by Jesus, "Well done, good and faithful servant" (Matthew 25:21) as we walk into eternity is the hope that has strengthened and inspired centuries of Christians to endure hardships for the gospel's sake. What we sometimes miss are the blessings that come *in this life* from suffering. "Blessed are you when people hate you and when they exclude you and revile you and spurn your name as evil, on account of the Son of Man!" Jesus says. "Rejoice in that day, and leap for joy, for behold, your reward is great in heaven; for so their fathers did to the prophets"

(Luke 6:22–23 ESV). What Jesus means in saying "blessed are you" in this passage and those like it is not only about a deferred hope. As Kenneth Bailey points out, the Greek word translated as "blessed" is *makarios*, and it is not meant to convey a wish for something that has yet to come; rather, *makarios* affirms *"a quality of spirituality that is already present."*[2]

In Luke 6:22–23, Jesus combines the deferred hope of the afterlife with a rich spirituality that suffering surprisingly secures for us now. In Mark 10:29–30, Jesus similarly tells us that persecution accompanies blessings "in this present age." Allow me to spotlight here the blessings that come in this life when we willingly suffer for Jesus' name's sake. "Christians are never urged to seek suffering; they are, however, encouraged to recognize that suffering is an extraordinary teacher" writes Bailey.[3] What suffering teaches us is that three blessings flow from its tutelage: (1) the blessing of an amplified testimony, (2) the blessing of a fulfilled identity, and (3) the blessing of unshakable faith and strength that never drains away.

THE BLESSING OF AN AMPLIFIED TESTIMONY

In his classic work *The Problem of Pain*, C. S. Lewis wrote that "God whispers to us in our pleasure, speaks in our conscience, but shouts in our pain: it is His megaphone to rouse a deaf world."[4] Lewis's observation is profound on so many levels.

We usually ask "Why?" after we've suffered some terrible loss. We look for a reason in it. It's as if our bodies can't contain the angst, and we feel some measure of relief when our mouths and breath form the question. What's fascinating is that we seldom ask "Why?" in our pleasures or successes. Yes, we may marvel occasionally at our fortune, but we seldom try to understand how our pleasure fits into some grand plan. For some reason, we passively accept blessings but struggle to make our sufferings mean something. Pain has a way of amplifying our awareness better than perhaps anything else.

Jesus told his disciples that the inevitable persecution they would suffer "will lead to an opportunity for your testimony" (Luke 21:13 NASB). We don't dare gloss over this remarkable gem. Indeed, one could write an entire book just on how this idea can and should shape our lives.

This all becomes very personal very quickly. Jesus wasn't talking only about pain in the abstract, as if it happens to people in faraway lands at the hands of faceless governments. Indeed, for the Easterner and Middle Easterner, Jesus made the point even sharper by bringing family into the equation. "But you will be betrayed even by parents and brothers and relatives and friends, and they will put some of you to death," he warned (Luke 21:16 NASB). I venture to say that it is one thing for a believer to stand firm in the face of self-righteous religious leaders or an unfamiliar cadre of secret police demanding the renunciation of faith. It's quite another for a believer to stand before a family member.

This is why Jesus mentioned family among those who may confront a new Christian. In his collectivist Middle Eastern context, family ties are virtually unbreakable. By saying that they will be so severely broken, Jesus put a sharp edge on the suffering that would follow a conversion. This illuminates an oft-misunderstood statement Jesus made: "I have not come to bring peace, but a sword" (Matthew 10:34 ESV). This has been misinterpreted by some to suggest that Jesus condoned religiously motivated violence. The sword Jesus referred to, however, is one that divides familial bonds—fathers from sons, mothers from daughters—not one that divides flesh and bone (verse 35).

Jesus knows that people will separate over who he is. This is made clear by the immediately preceding verses, where Jesus says, "So everyone who acknowledges me before men, I also will acknowledge before my Father who is in heaven" (verse 32 ESV). Jesus understands rejection all too well. As God incarnate, Jesus was rejected by his very creation, which led to the cross. The cross is where Jesus' testimony about the power and love of God was amplified. As they tortured him to death, Jesus prayed, "Father, forgive them, for they do not know what they are doing" (Luke 23:34). At the cross, a dying thief went from mocking Jesus (Matthew 27:44) to trusting Jesus with his eternal soul. Jesus forgave the sins of a dying thief, even as he himself was dying (Luke 23:39–43). So powerful a testimony was Jesus' suffering that pagan Roman soldiers recognized him as the Son of God (Matthew 27:54; Luke 23:47). Out of Jesus' anguish, the gospel message thundered in the ears of those who otherwise would have ignored him as just another religious teacher.

Jesus' disciples took up his mantle of suffering so that others might hear a message to which they would otherwise be deaf (see Acts 5). The apostle Paul's life was characterized by physical and emotional suffering resulting from his proclamation of the gospel. Consider Paul's words, written from a prison cell: "And most of the brothers, having become confident in the Lord by my imprisonment, are much more bold to speak the word without fear" (Philippians 1:14 ESV).

Does this not strike us as odd upon first reading it? Aren't shackles and jails meant to discourage the punished behavior, not encourage it? Why should Paul's imprisonments encourage anyone to boldly preach the same gospel that got Paul thrown in jail? The reality is that it did in Paul's day, and the church exploded for three hundred years because of the believers' chains.

Easterners and Middle Easterners admire convictions of faith, even if they try to suppress it with persecution. For centuries, Shi'a Muslims have commemorated the martyrdoms of Muhammad's grandson Hussein and his followers at Karbala as exemplars of strong faith. Easterners take notice when people willingly suffer for their faith. When followers of Christ suffer for their beliefs, they are blessed with the opportunity to testify to the power of the gospel.

Suffering for one's faith perks up Western ears and hearts just as well. Very recently, a young woman stood in line to meet me after a talk I gave. She had heard me speak a year or two earlier at a youth-oriented event. "Two things you said literally saved my life," she let out in tender tones. She pulled out the very notebook she had used that day and read out loud what I had said. "The cost of truth is worth paying," and "The answers are not hard to find, but they are hard to accept." I had said those words during a talk in which I used my own journey of faith as the backdrop, illustrating that truth often comes with a high personal price tag, but the benefits always outweigh the cost. "I was going to try to kill myself," she revealed. Indeed, she had attempted suicide on other occasions and fully intended to finish the job this time. "But your story and what you said stopped me. I'm alive today because of that." I firmly believe it wasn't what I said that impacted her heart. I said many things when she heard me speak years before. What she remembered, and what God used to amplify the gospel's effect on this young woman, was my willingness to endure pain for the sake of my faith.

I am of the firm conviction that suffering persecution is one of the most powerful ways to leave an impression on a person. Let me be clear, however. Suffering for one's faith doesn't prove anything is true. And in no way am I encouraging Christians to seek out persecution or to stop trying to end the gross suffering in our world. What I am saying is that God uses suffering to bless those who suffer with a credibility they might not otherwise have. That credibility reaches out beyond the believer who suffers. I have heard more people than I can remember tell me how reading Nabeel Qureshi's story helped them see the beauty of the gospel.

THE BLESSING OF A
FULFILLED IDENTITY

. . . that I may know him and the power of his resurrection, and may share his sufferings, becoming like him in his death.

PHILIPPIANS 3:10 ESV

One testimony that would otherwise not be fully heard, absent suffering, is the testimony of a fulfilled identity. Identifying with Christ means so much more than being in a particular tribe or club called Christianity. It means looking more and more like the one after whom the tribe is named. We are to express compassion as Christ did. We are to breach social barriers as he did. Perhaps most identity-defining of all, we are to suffer as he did. Strangely, paradoxically, springing up from that suffering is the joy of an identity that nothing but suffering for Jesus' sake can forge in us.

The New Testament book of Acts records the earliest days of the Christian movement—its triumphs and sufferings, its disputes and ultimate clarity. In Acts 5, we read that Jesus' disciples, emboldened by having seen the resurrected Jesus, began to preach in the streets, led by Peter. The same religious authorities who opposed Jesus violently opposed his disciples. They had Peter and the disciples beaten and thrown into prison. We read a curious description of what those same disciples did upon their release: "So they went on their way from the presence of the Council, rejoicing that they had been considered worthy to suffer shame for His name" (Acts 5:41 NASB).

What an amazing juxtaposition of old and new identities! The disciples, being Middle Eastern, would have tried to avoid public shame as much as possible. In the time after Jesus' execution and before his resurrection, they did just that, hiding in locked rooms. Yet we read that after seeing the raised Jesus, they didn't begrudgingly bear shame for Jesus' sake; they actually rejoiced in it. Why? Because they finally knew Jesus and what he was all about. Because they realized that identity in Christ meant bearing the same kind of shame their Savior bore. Their identities as honor-seeking religionists were being replaced with identities as humility-hungry servants.

May I suggest that this transformation is evidence of divine intervention in the lives of these men? Peter originally wanted the glory of dying for Jesus in a sword fight. He eventually coveted the honor of identifying with the humiliated Christ. Paul's complete turnaround is similar evidence of divine intervention. Paul described looking like Christ as so luminous an attainment that all other blessings and treasures were dim by comparison. "Indeed, I count everything as loss because of the surpassing worth of knowing Christ Jesus my Lord. For his sake I have suffered the loss of all things and count them as rubbish, in order that I may gain Christ and be found in him" (Philippians 3:8–9 ESV). The accolades and honor of being counted as a legally faultless and pious Jew were nothing—less than nothing—compared to knowing Jesus. And what did it mean to know Jesus? Paul answers: "that I may know him and the power of his resurrection, and may share his sufferings, becoming like him in his death" (verse 10 ESV).

In the West, where it has been relatively comfortable to call oneself a Christian, it may be hard to fathom this truth. I recall hearing the story of a theologian who was visiting American churches for the first time. After a multistate tour, one of his hosts asked him what he thought of American Christianity. His response was something like this: "Very impressive. Your buildings are vast, and your worship is passionate. But there seems to be no room in your theology for suffering."

I'm convinced that his statement wasn't meant as a chastisement, but as a lament that American Christians are missing out on the gift—yes, the gift—of suffering. Seeing suffering for the gospel as a gift comes not from wild speculation but from the authority of Scripture. As Paul faced his fate and looked back on a life of suffering for the gospel's sake, he was inspired to write, "For it has been *granted* to you that for the sake of Christ you should not only believe in him but also suffer for his sake" (Philippians 1:29 ESV, emphasis mine). The word *granted* comes from the Greek word *echaristhe*, which means "to give something as a sign of one's beneficent goodwill toward someone" or "to graciously give to another."[5] How gloriously strange! It has been lavishly given to each Christian—as a sign of God's beneficent goodwill—that we might suffer for his name's sake. The suffering in and of itself isn't the gift; identifying with Jesus is.

Any Christian experience devoid of identifying with Christ in this way is a shallower experience. Dallas Willard reportedly quipped that some people are "vampire" Christians—they want Jesus only for his blood.[6] Once they have salvation, they make Jesus their cosmic lifeguard, not the Lord of their lives. "Vampire Christian" isn't so much an insult as it is a sad description of those who lack the depth of what it means to be "in Christ."

This understanding dovetails beautifully with Luke's account in Acts 5 that the disciples rejoiced at the gift of suffering the same kind of shame that Jesus suffered. They realized the gift they had been given—true identity in Christ. Is this beautiful poetry not enough to give us pause? Recall that shame is the ultimate negative reinforcement in Eastern and Middle Eastern cultures. Yet Jesus' Middle Eastern followers discovered that it was through public shaming that they were given the honor of identifying with the Son of God.

Recall also that in Eastern and Middle Eastern contexts, honor and shame are about *who* you are, not just what you do. That means that removal of shame takes more than mere penance. It takes a new identity. Jesus' followers were so soaked in the honor of identifying with him that heaps of shame from the authorities resulted not in groans but in rejoicing.

THE BLESSING OF UNSHAKABLE FAITH AND STRENGTH THAT NEVER DRAINS AWAY

I recently participated in a dialogue with a prominent atheist philosopher at a major university. Toward the end of our cordial time together, the moderator asked us to share what we admired most about the other person's position. My counterpart paused before answering. He then said he envied the unshakable assurance and certainty of Christian faith that he could never have as a philosopher, since he is burdened with basing his beliefs on evidence, which makes them subject to change. It was a backhanded compliment to be sure, at once envying a Christian's assurance while simultaneously suggesting that such assurance only came through unexamined faith. Though his assumption about the Christian faith being unthinking was wrong, I believe his envy of Christian assurance was sincere. Yet many Christians remain assured and unshakable in their faith precisely *because* the evidence for their faith is so strong.

Indeed, many a Christian's evidence-based faith has withstood more than just counterarguments. The faith of the twenty-one Coptic Christians withstood the horrors of ISIS on the Mediterranean shore. God's glory shone through those men because their amplified testimonies and fulfilled identities in Christ coalesced into the third blessing—that of an unshakable faith.

Scripture's depth astounds me whenever my heart lingers over what happened to those twenty-one men. "I can do all things through him who strengthens me," Paul writes in Philippians 4:13 (ESV). The faithful cling to those words when hanging from a cliff of difficult circumstances. More than once I've prayed those words as I stood on the cusp of some anxiety-inducing situation. They are comforting, empowering words. Christians have heard them preached hundreds of times. Big-name athletes have quoted them after overcoming the odds on athletic fields. There are times, however, when someone lives out such an oft-quoted passage in a gust of faith that lifts the fog of our familiarity and illuminates a fuller meaning. Those twenty-one men did exactly that.

In the embers of our outrage over their executions, and the executions of journalists and foreign aid workers before and since, we may think that if we were in that situation, we'd face our death with William Wallace–style defiance. The reality is that such bravery is normally elusive and illusory.

An article about how a certain country metes out capital punishment through public beheadings describes the surprising fact that the condemned tend not to fight, even as they walk to the spot where their lives will end. They simply kneel or lie down, surrendering to their fate. No matter how hardened the criminal might be, "Their strength drains away," the country's chief executioner reported.[7] They have no fight left in them. That's why ISIS's victims have often seemed so strangely passive in the moments before the imminent brutality. When faced with death, our hearts melt. Our knees buckle. Our "strength drains away."

But appearances can be deceiving. The strength of those twenty-one Coptic Christians did not drain away. They should have melted before their captors' ravenous barbarity. Mere human strength normally does drain away in that situation. Yet the Christians refused to renounce Christ to save their lives and instead called on him, knowing that doing so would end their lives. They did the remarkable for one reason: they could do all things through Christ who gave them a strength that does not drain away.

What Jesus—the one whom Arab Christians call *Yesua*—did through these men enriches our understanding of Philippians 4:13's words. We rely on that verse in adversity-ridden times with the expectation that things eventually will work out in our favor. Those men have taught us that the words mean much more. *Yesua* strengthens us incredibly when we are faced with the incredible. We can do *all* things, including standing strong even when we know we will not be delivered from our earthly trouble.

We'd like to think we could look into the eyes of our would-be executioners and profess Christ. But if we're genuinely reflective, we wonder whether we really would. Yet this is what I've learned from twenty-one men I've never met: *I could do it through Christ who gives me strength.* Their faithfulness in the face of terror has revolutionized how I see Paul's familiar words to the Philippians. For that, I am eternally grateful to them and to the God who gave them the strength.

MORE THAN CONQUERORS

These twenty-one Christians taught me to see another commonly quoted verse afresh as well. Paul writes that "in all these things we are more than conquerors through him who loved us" (Romans 8:37). Westerners tend to quote these words triumphalistically. Neither Satan nor any challenge life can throw at us has a chance because we are the conquerors of conquerors.

But what about those faithful Egyptian Christians? They were not delivered from the physical pain, terror, and ultimate tragedies plotted against them by murderous thugs. Were they not more than conquerors?

Yes, and in a way that surpasses our common understanding. Consider the context of Paul's words in Romans 8:37. We are more than conquerors through Christ as we face our troubles, including persecution and even death (verse 35). And he tells us that not even death can separate us from the love of Christ (verses 38–39). It is in that—the inseverable love of Yesua—that we are more than conquerors, even when it appears we've been conquered. Had those men renounced their faith in Yesua, they would have been conquered.

The cowardly radicals thought they had conquered the Christian men simply because they had them on their knees. Yet those very same Christians were more than ISIS's conquerors because they cleaved to Yesua even in the face of the unspeakable. Each one of them was something more than a conqueror—something different than and better than a conqueror—because they emulated the One they professed to love with their final breaths.

PAIN FOR CHRIST'S SAKE

Caesar had no army to match the angel armies of Yahweh. Yet Yesua did not sound the charge as he was dragged to court and brutalized and crucified. He came to give his life as a ransom for many. How ironic that Yesua sacrificed himself to give eternal life to the very people who sought his death! Like those twenty-one men, Yesua faced a terrible and inevitable pain at the hands of sin's ugliness. Yet he did not lose heart, and his strength did not drain away. He endured the cross because of the joy set before him—the salvation of those who don't deserve his mercy but trust him for it. Jesus is more than a conqueror over sinners; he is a transformer of sinners into saints.

This is what it truly means to be able to do *all* things through Christ who strengthens us and to be *more* than conquerors. We can have the strength to do all things, including enduring the unspeakable, because we have Christ in us. Yesua gives us strength that does not drain away.

In the martyrs' actions, we see vividly the blessings that follow pain for the gospel's sake. There is the blessing of an amplified testimony. Those twenty-one men spoke to millions more in their deaths than they ever could have in their lives. There is the blessing of a fulfilled identity. Just as Paul identified with Christ in his suffering and his death, so did those twenty-one men. They knelt before masked murderers who were literally clothed in darkness. The men were clothed in bright orange jumpsuits, meant to look like prisoners, even though they were the ones who were truly free. Because of their bright jumpsuits, those Christians, not their murderers, catch our eyes. Because those men called out to Jesus in their last moments, it is him we see through them. How amazing. Their testimony was amplified so that their identity in Christ was magnified and their unshakeable faith was solidified. In all of this, God was glorified.

If shame is most feared in an Eastern mind-set, honor is most cherished. Radicals tried to put those men to shame, and yet the perseverance of their faith brought them honor. "In this you rejoice," Peter writes to those suffering indignity for the sake of their faith, "though now for a little while, if necessary, you have been grieved by various trials, so that the tested genuineness of your faith—more precious than gold that perishes though it is tested by fire—may be found to result in praise and glory and honor at the revelation of Jesus Christ" (1 Peter 1:6–7 ESV).

Critics have argued that Paul invented much of what is today's Christianity and that he taught something diametrically opposed to other apostles like James. James, so the argument goes, seems to teach that salvation and justification before God come primarily by our good works (James 2:14–17). Paul, on the other hand, teaches that we are justified by faith alone apart from works (Ephesians 2:8–9). The most direct response is that James didn't teach that we are justified by works. Rather, he taught that "faith without works is dead," meaning that a living, saving faith would result in good works and that good works are the proof that we have faith (James 2:18). Paul teaches exactly the same principle (Ephesians 2:10).

Yet another response is to point not only to specific consistencies between James and Paul, but to general consistencies as well. In his letter, James teaches that Christians are to count it "joy" when faced with trials due to our faith because such trials lead to perseverance and spiritual character (James 1:2–4). Couple this with Paul's teaching in Romans 5:3 that Christians are to "rejoice" in sufferings because they produce endurance, character, and hope. James and Paul consistently teach the central role that faith in Christ has in not only *saving* a person's soul, but also in *shaping* a person's soul. The hope that is produced "does not put us to shame," Paul writes (verse 5). Rather it forges an honorable character.

These are the blessings that await all of us if we find ourselves sheltered in Christ. We may never face a terrible trial for our faith. It is likely that those twenty-one men never thought they would either. Many of us wonder if we would have the strength to faithfully endure suffering for Christ's sake. We will never truly know until we've been tested. In the meantime, we can rest in the fact that those twenty-one men weren't actually extraordinary. They just relied on the One who is.

Chapter 6

PARABLES

Teaching Truth through Eastern Immersion

Abdu Murray

Almost every lesson I've learned about life from my family had a parable or colorfully worded proverb attached to it. When my father would teach us what it meant to be married, he would tell the parable of two brothers in ancient Arabia whose marriages turned out vastly different, based on how the men provided for their families. Even today, whenever I go to buy a pair of shoes, I can hear in my head an Arabic saying—*Al-ghali a-rakhis*—literally, "The expensive is cheap." The saying conveys the idea that spending money up front on a quality product avoids having to pay double to replace a cheaper one. Somehow the cleverly worded idiom "the expensive is cheap" preserves the wisdom better than a lengthier explanation.

Eastern communication is delightfully dressed in idioms and parables. Yet this isn't so foreign to Western communication, is it? After all, Westerners have fables teaching that hard work pays off ("The Little Red Hen"), that appearances can be dangerously deceiving ("Little Red Riding Hood"), and that other people's property ought to be respected ("Goldilocks and the Three Bears"). I have a particularly vivid memory of unsuccessfully trying to play a prank on my mother by scaring her into thinking my younger brother had an accident (ketchup across the neck was involved), only to have her tell me the horrifying—and quite effective—story of the little boy who cried wolf.

Some have said that sophisticated ideas and propositions are too big for parables and proverbs. They are good for children's lessons or for less intellectually developed times in our history. But today, especially in the post-Enlightenment West, we've outgrown such teaching devices. Describing Western thought processes, Brandon O'Brien and E. Randolph Richards observe, "To us, things like metaphors and parables sometimes seem like unnecessarily frilly packages for a hard truth. We want to get past the packaging to the content; we want to know what it *means*."[1] It has been argued that Jesus' use of parables was helpful for farmers and shepherds who didn't have a grasp of logic and syllogisms but that he isn't sophisticated enough for modern sensibilities. Such an argument plays to the Western tendency to see parables and illustrations as mere window dressing or as packaging that at best helps us understand a point being made but at worst obfuscates the illogic.

I recall asking a close friend what he didn't like about Christianity, and he said it encourages conformity and lazy thinking. "The sheep metaphors are pretty obviously encouraging people to be loyal automatons," he said. His statement was fascinating for a couple of reasons.

First, it downplays the fact that Jesus' use of shepherds and sheep as metaphors in the first-century Middle East made his message of God's sacrificial love for humanity all the more relatable to the agrarian people Jesus encountered. Shepherds knew the sacrifices it took to tend sheep and thus could better understand God's concern for humanity through that lens. Jewish shepherds would also be struck by the fact that Jesus himself was referred to as a sacrificial lamb. In other words, calling someone a sheep was never meant to be an insult because it is the very metaphor God uses to describe himself at times. Jesus' use of sheep as a metaphor for both humanity and for God achieves clarity on both topics with an elegance that's hard to achieve with dry syllogisms. As Kenneth Bailey says, it's a mistake to relegate Jesus to a "village rustic creating folktales for fisherman and farmers" because examining his parables with care shows them to be "serious theology."[2] While it may be true that simplistic tales like "Goldilocks" and "The Little Red Hen" have limited value, the same isn't true of Jesus' parables.

Second, the very fact that my friend had a reaction to the Bible's sheep metaphors shows that metaphors communicate quite powerfully to Western minds as well as to Eastern minds. He missed out on the metaphors' depth simply because he failed to actually study them. Yet the imagery endured in his Western mind.

Before we plumb the depths of Jesus' serious theology found in parables, let's pause for a moment to give logic and evidence their due respect. Parables or illustrations aren't substitutes for well-reasoned arguments or evidence. This is true across all cultures. After all, a parable is only as useful as the logic behind it. Good parables, however, beef up an argument's thrust by making it relatable and mentally sticky. Parables based on sound logic do more than just teach us propositional truths. They employ characters and themes that immerse us into the truths being taught. They force us to ask how we would act in a situation and whether the truth really matters to us. I once heard my colleague Christian Hofreiter comment that if we don't see ourselves in Jesus' parables, we've missed the point. If it's true that Westerners want to know what a truth means, parables reach deeper to show how a truth applies.

Parables don't just teach us truth, therefore; they also teach us about our relationship to the truth. Jesus' parables have touched Easterners and Westerners alike, because through them he invites us into a relationship with truth itself.

MINING PARABLES FOR LINGERING LOGIC

Describing the depths of Jesus' many parables would take far more space than a single chapter in a book like this allows. Others have written chapters on each parable, and I'd venture to say that a multivolume book could scarcely exhaust the subject. Here I want to summarize a few of Jesus' parables to show the amazing ways in which they profoundly convey truth but also answer some of the thorniest objections to Christianity.

Is Christianity Intolerantly Exclusive?
The Parable of the Banquet

Food is one of my love languages. My wife and I were recently discussing how some say that music or mathematics are universal languages. We both beg to differ. It's food that speaks to all people. Those who know my affinity for culinary quality (and, unfortunately, quantity) will chuckle to see that the first parable I've chosen to focus on is Jesus' parable of the great banquet recorded in Luke 14:15–24.

Jesus tells the story of a wealthy man who had prepared a great banquet and invited many to come. Rather than accept the generous invitation, various invitees offered lame excuses for not showing up (Luke 14:18–20). The master then instructed his servants to go into the streets and invite the poor and those with physical infirmities to enjoy the bounty. Even after they came, there was still room at the table for more guests. That's when the master gave his servants a subtly remarkable imperative: "*Go out* to the highways and hedges and *compel* people to come in, that my house may be filled" (verse 23 ESV, emphasis mine). That the master wants his house to be filled is a small detail to which we'll return, because of its tremendous significance.

The master gives progressively inclusive invitations. That's quintessential Middle Eastern hospitality. Middle Eastern guest lists aren't nearly as selective as those in the West. There are no assigned tables or seats. It was true in Jesus' day, and it's still true today. I recall many occasions when I was younger seeing invitations to weddings that were addressed to my father "and his family." Sometimes there was no written invitation; just a phone call or an impromptu visit to convey the request. The hosts assumed that all of us, regardless of our ages, would come to the reception. There was no concern about whether we'd fill up a table or need extra place settings. That would all be sorted out later. What was important was that the banquet hall would be full so that the community could share in the bliss. I felt a sense of adulthood the first time I received an invitation to a Lebanese wedding addressed to "Mr. Abdu Murray and his family." The lack of specificity was a warm sign of respect. (As an aside, if you're ever invited to attend a Lebanese wedding, do yourself the favor of going.)

The context in which Jesus delivered the parable of the great banquet helps us understand why the little phrase "so that my house may be filled" mustn't escape our attention. Jesus spoke this parable while he was a dinner guest at someone's home. As he was speaking, someone declared, "Blessed is everyone who will eat bread in the kingdom of God!" (verse 15 ESV). Seizing on the opportunity to explain who "everyone" includes, Jesus told this parable. The master in the parable is obviously a proxy for God, who invites people of every stature to enjoy his hospitality. Why does God invite everyone? So "that my house may be filled," Jesus answers (verse 23 ESV).

This short phrase funnels the parable's many lessons into a response to the common objection that Christianity is intolerantly exclusive. Claiming that faith in Christ is the only means of salvation is increasingly unpopular. Many argue that Christianity unnecessarily excludes people from heaven just because they don't happen to believe a particular idea. This objection misses the "good news" aspect of the gospel message altogether. Salvation in Christianity isn't about believing the right thing; it's about trusting the right person to lift us out of the muck of sin. We can trust in ourselves, in trying to please God, in the Brahman, or in whatever force we ascribe divinity to, or we can trust in Jesus—the only one who proved himself to be qualified to pay our debts for us. No, God doesn't send people to hell because they believe the wrong thing. People separate themselves from God because of their moral choices and the rejection of the invitation that God has given to be reconciled to him.

The fact that the master in the parable (God) invites everyone to his banquet so that his house may be filled shows that God has indeed provided an exclusive means of salvation, but his invitation to accept that salvation is as inclusive as it could be. There will be those who know they need a savior but still reject that savior. There will be others who feel themselves so undeserving of a savior that they hardly believe they've been invited into God's house. God sends his servants to urge such people—to "compel" them—to accept his invitation. They, like so many of us, will come and fill God's house.

In this single parable, we are treated to a variety-laden banquet. We are taught lessons about pride. We are taught lessons about honor and shame. We are taught lessons about the heart of God. And we are taught that God's invitation has no place cards and no VIP passes.

Seeking Labor, Finding Compassion: The Parable of the Workers in the Vineyard

Having spent most of my life in a religious system that taught that the heavenly paradise is earned through good works, I was quite resistant to the "good news" that God grants salvation to us through unmerited grace. It isn't only the Muslim or religiously observant Jew who finds the biblical idea of grace difficult to swallow. My many conversations with people raised in the West who ascribe to "good personism"— the belief that if one tries hard to be a good person, God will grant entry into heaven—have shown that grace isn't as easily accepted as one might expect.

For me, the logic of the good news eventually settled in my mind. A perfectly holy God cannot compromise his maximal justice for the sake of forgiveness. But a maximally compassionate God mustn't forego forgiveness to adhere to justice. This creates a seeming dilemma: my wrongdoing must be addressed if God is to be maximally just, but salvation only comes when God forgives. How then can maximal justice and maximal forgiveness be achieved without compromising either? The cross, where Jesus voluntarily pays my debt of sin on my behalf, is the place where justice is served and mercy is granted.

This logic sticks best in the Eastern mind through story. In Matthew 20:1–16, Jesus offers a rich parable of what it means for God to be merciful to broken humanity in a way that also affords us the dignity of God taking our actions seriously.

In this parable, a vineyard owner goes out early in the morning with the intention of hiring laborers for his land. It was customary in those days (and in some places today) for day laborers to gather at a certain location in hopes that those needing hired hands would pick them. The vineyard owner hires certain men and comes to an agreement on wages—a denarius for a day's work (verse 2). Later, the vineyard owner returns a second time and sees men whom he did not originally hire still waiting for work. So he employs them as well. He comes back a third, fourth, and even fifth time, each time finding willing laborers there waiting to be hired. The fact that those men waited all day for work showed their eagerness to work.

With every passing hour, the honor of providing for their families was fading into the shame of returning home to their wives and children in failure. The Middle Easterners hearing Jesus' parable would have picked up that element of the story immediately. They also would have picked up on the fact that the vineyard owner hires the last of the laborers at the last hour of the workday. He could have had pity on those men and just given them some money. In that case, the men would have had to tell their families that they had received charity instead of work. Instead, the vineyard owner offers them a job, even if only for an hour. He affords them the dignity of being able to tell their families that they had been useful, that what they did mattered. Again, that decision wouldn't have been lost on Jesus' audience.

The parable takes a bit of a surprising turn, however. At the end of the day, the master of the vineyard (Jesus switches from calling him *the owner* to *the master*) pays all the workers the same wage, irrespective of how long they've been working for him. Those he hired in the morning got the denarius they agreed on, and those hired with just an hour to work were paid the same amount (verses 8–9). Those who were hired first see this and protest. They worked all day in the hot sun, after all; shouldn't they be paid more than those who worked only an hour?

The first time I read this parable, I was a Muslim and I recall thinking that the Christian who directed me to it must not have read it himself. *How unjust!* I mentally yelled. *This Christian wants me to believe that this unfairness is how salvation works?* Allowing the parable to marinate in the olive oil and lemon juice of the Middle East eventually brought out its true flavors.

The vineyard master counters the objection of those hired first marvelously. "Friend, I am doing you no wrong. Did you not agree with me for a denarius? Take what belongs to you and go. I choose to give to this last worker as I give to you. Am I not allowed to do what I choose with what belongs to me? Or do you begrudge my generosity?" (verses 13–15 ESV). There is so much depth to plumb in his words, but let's focus our lens on just a couple of aspects to see the import of Jesus' lesson.

First, Jesus uses the parable to address the perpetual paradox of human free will interacting with God's sovereignty. One of the most frequently asked questions I receive at open forums is, "If God knows and controls everything, how are human beings free or responsible for their actions?" It is a deep question to be sure, but we mustn't forget that it presents a paradox, not a contradiction. Everyone, regardless of their beliefs, has to wrestle with some version of this paradox. Indeed, I believe that in a naturalistic worldview, human free will actually poses a contradiction.

During a dialogue I had with an atheist professor, the first question the moderator asked us was, "Are we determined or free?" Fascinatingly, the professor responded that he found the question uninteresting. But surely it's very interesting, because the answer tells us much about what kind of creatures we are and whether we actually arrive at truths through logic and inference. If we are just complex chemical machines, we don't employ logic and reasoning. We just respond to external stimuli based on our biochemistry. In other words, there is no free will.

Toward the end of the dialogue, that same professor said something along the lines of "I find the idea of God having a plan for my life or being in control repugnant." *Wait a minute!* I thought. *How could it be repugnant for God to determine the paths of our lives if it's "uninteresting" whether humans are free or determined?* He certainly found the question interesting enough when God entered the picture. Absent God, human free will is an illusion at best and our assertion that it exists is a contradiction, not a paradox. In God, the problem is only a paradox. Jesus refused to punt on the question and instead used this parable to address it.

The workers at the beginning of the day used their free will to *agree* on the one denarius as their wage. The men who waited all day for work could have gone home at any time but *chose* to linger there in hopes of getting work. At the same time, the vineyard master exercised his authority to *pick* whom he would hire. In fact, in the first round, he went out with the specific purpose of hiring laborers for the vineyard. Jesus purposefully uses language showing that in subsequent hiring rounds, the master simply went out and "saw" men standing around waiting for work. The master again exercised his sovereignty to hire more workers, perhaps even more than he needed. Human free will was on display in that the men chose how to spend their day.

God's sovereignty was exercised in that the master chose whom to hire and what to pay. How such free will and sovereignty work is the paradox. That they work together is on display in a dance that our limited lenses cannot fully observe this side of heaven.

Second, we learn something about God's delight in responding to faith and honoring those who might feel ashamed. The men who stood around all day waiting for work had very little reason to do so. It was typical for business owners and landowners to hire people only once—in the morning. It would be uncommon for someone to get hired in the middle of the day or once it was past noon. Even then, only one or two people may get hired if someone from the morning got injured or sick. Thus, most day laborers would have gone home disappointed right after the first (and usually only) round of hiring.

The fact that the vineyard master found men still eager to work at the end of the day told him something about their faith. Yes, they faced the shame of standing around all day but held out hope that they wouldn't have to face the greater shame of going home empty-handed. I wonder if Jesus meant to communicate through this parable that the men's daylong faith was credited to them as daylong work.

The mind naturally turns to Abraham, who lived centuries before. Though Abraham was childless, God promised him a son who would become a great nation and through whom the Savior of the world would come. Abraham waited years for that promise to be fulfilled in the birth of Isaac, and he did not live to witness the Savior's birth. Yet "[he] believed the LORD, and he credited it to him as righteousness" (Genesis

15:6; see Romans 4:3). That kind of faith shifts our usual selfward focus Godward.

The workers hired at the end of the day received their pay gratefully. Notice, however, that the men hired in the morning didn't protest that the men hired later should have been paid *less*; they demanded to get paid *more* than they had agreed on (verse 10). Their selfward gaze obscured their view of God's generous grace. The men who held out hope to avoid shame were ultimately honored by the vineyard master. How characteristically Eastern of Jesus to use the honor-shame paradigm in the form of an Eastern parable to teach the universal truth of God's love.

Some have said that Jesus' parable of the workers in the vineyard teaches salvation by good works. Still others object that this teaches something immoral—that those who have lived a life of selfishness and have deathbed conversions are unjustly rewarded as if they lived selfless lives of service to humanity. This parable addresses all of those arguments and supports none of them. Instead, it teaches us that faith— actively trusting God—is rewarded by a God who is worthy of that trust. The men who waited around for work were not using their time on selfish pursuits. They didn't say, "Oh well, maybe tomorrow," and then head off to get drunk or carouse with prostitutes. No, they trusted and waited in hope. Jesus teaches us that heaven is not going to be a place of petty jealousies. Instead, we will all be like those workers who were hired last, having no reason to boast in our efforts before a generous God. We are to be grateful, understanding that none of us are deserving of his generosity. Perhaps living in that hope now will make us act less petty on this side of heaven.

The Heart of Man and the Heart of God:
The Parable of the Good Samaritan

A great example of a parable that teaches with power and poetry is Jesus' famous parable of the good Samaritan (Luke 10:25–37). Let's be cautious not to allow our familiarity with the parable to obscure a fresh view of its truths.

The phrase "good Samaritan" is common across a wide spectrum of subcultures, Christian and otherwise. We often hear people refer to someone who stops to give unexpected aid as a good Samaritan. I've seen roadside assistance vans traversing the freeways with "Good Samaritan" emblazoned on their side panels. It's fascinating that we've come to associate the word *Samaritan* with heroism and virtue. In Jesus' day, however, Samaritans were hated by Jews (and they hated Jews right back), because Samaritans were seen as ethnic half-breeds and religious compromisers. Jesus used that cultural and religious hostility to teach a lesson as rich as a multi-layered cake.

Jesus told the parable of the good Samaritan in response to a lawyer's public challenge. The lawyer asked Jesus, "What must I do to inherit eternal life?" (Luke 10:25). Jesus asked the legal expert what the law itself says. Responding as a lawyer would, he quoted the law: "'Love the Lord your God with all your heart and with all your soul and with all your strength and with all your mind'; and, 'Love your neighbor as yourself'" (verse 27; see Deuteronomy 6:5; Leviticus 19:18). Jesus turned the tables on the lawyer. "You have answered correctly," Jesus replied. "Do this and you will live" (verse 28). Remember, the lawyer had challenged Jesus with a legal question. Jesus doesn't answer, but responds by asking the lawyer what the law says. When the lawyer quotes the law, Jesus says that *the lawyer* answered correctly. But it was the lawyer who was trying to get an answer out of Jesus! Speaking as a trial attorney myself, I can't help but smile at the head-spinning turnabout.

Perhaps realizing that he was losing control of the engagement, the lawyer follows up. "And who is my neighbor?" he retorts (verse 29). The legal expert asked Jesus for the meaning of the very law he just quoted. Jesus could have given a straightforward answer like, "Every person is your neighbor." That statement would have fallen flat at best or seemed ridiculous at worst to the ethnocentric mind-set of Jesus' day. Rather than give a legal definition, Jesus did something very Middle Eastern and told a parable.

He described a traveler who is beaten by robbers and left for dead. Along comes a priest, who passes by without helping the brutalized man. Next comes a Levite, a man who must remain ritually clean for his temple service. That similarly pious man similarly refuses to help. Jesus then tells how a third man—this one a Samaritan—has compassion for the victim, binds his wounds, takes him to an inn, and pays whatever it costs to heal the man. Jesus made a detested Samaritan the hero of the story. This is yet another turnabout.

The parable was, to put it mildly, scandalous to first-century Jewish ears. Jesus easily could have made Samaritans to be the ones who passed by without helping, and a pious Jew to be the hero. He flipped that script, as it were, and in doing so, he taught a couple of profound lessons with just a short story.

First, Jesus challenged the prejudices of his culture. Our

neighbors don't have to look like us, believe what we believe, or speak our language. Humanity is a global community, and each person is invested with dignity. The insidiousness of ethnic and racial animus is that it blinds us to our own sin. "They" are always the prejudiced ones, while "we" are always the victims. By making the stereotypically unsavory Samaritan the hero, Jesus challenges each of us to unveil the secret prejudices we may harbor against others. And he told the parable, not just to the self-seeking lawyer who challenged him, but to everyone within the sound of his voice. That included his own Samaritan-averse disciples.

Perhaps it's no accident that just days before this encounter with the lawyer, an entire Samaritan village rejected Jesus because he was Jewish and was headed toward the Jewish holy city of Jerusalem (Luke 9:51–56). Incensed at the lowly Samaritans' audacity, Jesus' disciples James and John sought divine vengeance. "Lord, do you want us to tell fire to come down from heaven and consume them?" they asked (verse 54 ESV). In a response that was surprising for that cultural climate, Jesus rebuked his disciples. He understood that judgment would eventually come for all who reject the One who could stand in their place before God, but Jesus wanted to give the Samaritans every chance to repent before that judgment would come. How humbling Jesus' parable of the Good Samaritan must have been to James and John. The parable teaches us all that, indeed, "God did not send his Son into the world to condemn the world, but in order that the world might be saved through him" (John 3:17 ESV).

As I reflect on the depth of what Jesus taught, I can't help but think of a comment an atheist made during a dialogue we participated in at a major university. During his opening remarks, the atheist speaker pointed out that he had been on the receiving end of jokes and insults from religious people because he was an atheist. A few minutes later, he brought up the parable of the good Samaritan and said he hated it. It fascinated me how such a bright man could miss the point of the parable by such a galactic margin. When my time to speak came, I couldn't help but say, "Of all the parables, this one should be your favorite. Jesus makes hyper-religious people the bad guys. If he were to give this parable today, he could just as easily have used an atheist to replace the Samaritan to prove his point." The man was so caught up in his disdain for Christianity that he failed to see what Jesus was really teaching us about the human heart.

The second lesson Jesus taught with this parable is more subtle but no less important. Kenneth Bailey makes the point that in making the Samaritan—an ethnic and religious outsider—the saving agent, Jesus taught that the Savior would "break in from the outside."[3] That is the incarnation of God in Christ. God breaks into human history by taking on human form, the form of a servant, to save us from each other and from ourselves. The fact that the Samaritan in Jesus' parable not only takes the man to an inn but also *pays* whatever it costs to heal him tells us about the costly sacrifice the Messiah makes for each of us, no matter who we are. "In this parable," Bailey writes, "the Samaritan extends a costly demonstration of unexpected love to the wounded man, and in the process Jesus again interprets the life-changing power of costly love that would climax at his cross."[4]

The more I study the nuance and artistry of this parable,

the more I'm convinced of its divine inspiration. A lawyer tries to trap Jesus in a legal thicket, only to have Jesus teach him the spirit of the law and the heart of the Lawgiver. Using a short story, Jesus teaches us to confront our own prejudices and see each other as God sees each of us. At the same time, by describing the good Samaritan as a stranger who redeems someone at great personal cost, Jesus reveals the character of the Messiah. Jesus teaches us about ourselves while simultaneously teaching us what God is like. Straightforward propositional statements can't reveal such truths with that much power and poetry. But parables can.

THE GOSPEL BY ACCIDENT

I have always been a movie lover. Stories as a means of conveying deep truths fascinate me. Perhaps it's my Middle Eastern blood. Maybe it's just part of being human. Eastern modes of teaching convey deep truths in the form of stories, but this seems no less true in the West, which is why the Middle Easterner from Nazareth appeals to us all, no matter how much melanin is in our skin.

I would dare say that the gospel message—the "good news"—is so powerful and so prevalent in the minds of Easterner and Westerner alike that we often tell it in whole or in part, even when we don't intend to. Of course, Christian themes and imagery have been intentionally used in works of literature, plays, and movies for centuries. From Charles Dickens's *A Tale of Two Cities* to *The Matrix* trilogy, creative writers have drawn inspiration from the message that humanity is in need of saving and saving only comes from a savior who gives of himself.

The novel *A Simple Plan* by Scott B. Smith—and the 1998 film adaptation of the same name—also draws on biblical themes, though it is not a particularly Christian book. The plot centers around three men who happen across a crashed plane buried in deep snow in the woods. They discover four and a half million dollars in the plane—and a dead body. The "simple plan" they hatch is that one of them will keep the money until the snow thaws. If there are any signs that someone is looking for the money, they will return it to the plane or to the authorities. If no one comes looking for it, the men will split the money evenly, leave town, and never see each other again. Of course, the simple plan gets complicated quickly because human greed and distrust set in. The men soon grow to distrust each other, and they commit a string of murders. People who would never have considered themselves capable of such atrocities find themselves unable to stop committing them.

After some friends and I left the theater, we engaged in a lively discussion about what we would have done if we had found the money. Like the characters in the film, we all fooled ourselves into thinking we wouldn't succumb to greed's power. The reality is that evil stalks every heart, and the right conditions can set it into motion. This is part of the Christian message, though not a pleasant part. What *A Simple Plan* does is make us face up to it. Like a good parable, the film drew each of us in to the lesson being taught.

While *A Simple Plan* stirred up ideas consistent with part of the gospel message, other movies without an overtly religious message have told much more of it. It may have surprised some to see this happen in the 2007 film *I Am Legend*. It's an adaptation of a 1954 novel of the same name, but it veers from the original story quite a bit.

In the 2007 film, a scientist mutates a virus to attack and kill cancer. After amazing success, things go terribly awry as the virus ends up killing 90 percent of humanity and turning the rest into cannibalistic creatures whose skin burns when exposed to sunlight. The only person immune to the virus is Robert Neville, a world-famous virologist.

The imagery is all there: Humanity is on the knife-edge of ruin. The remnants of us hate the light and are bent on killing the only person immune from the corruption. The only person immune also happens to be the only one capable of curing everyone's infection. At the end of the movie, Neville discovers a cure for the virus using his own blood. To get the blood into the right hands, however, he has to sacrifice his life.

This movie includes elements of the gospel story, of course. Humanity has been plagued by sin and now hates the light, loving the darkness more (John 3:19). Jesus, being God incarnate, was immune from sin but chose to live among us to point us to God. He alone has the cure to sin and gave his life, shedding his blood so that we can be free of what we've become through our own efforts. Thousands have seen *I Am Legend*, including those who may never crack open a Bible, yet a glimmer of its message has penetrated their world.

I remember being deeply touched by a scene in the film *Dead Man Walking*. The movie depicts Sister Helen Prejean's efforts to keep a convicted felon named Matthew Poncelet from being executed by lethal injection. When Prejean first meets Poncelet, he's sexist, racist, and angry. He refuses to admit he helped murder a young couple in the woods and rape the woman. Prejean's goal isn't just to keep Poncelet from dying. She is fiercely interested in his salvation. Eventually, her love and kindness affect Poncelet so profoundly that he confesses his part in the brutality. Nor have her efforts to introduce him to Jesus failed because he receives Christ as his Savior.

Her efforts to stop the execution do fail, however. The scene that touched me shows Poncelet fearfully shuddering as the minutes shrink closer to his execution. Poncelet urges Prejean to sing a hymn. Prejean protests that she's a terrible singer, but Poncelet wants to hear it anyway. With her face pressed between the cell bars as if she were trying to absorb her way in, she sings "Be Not Afraid"—a song that speaks of how Jesus faces reality's harshness alongside us.[5]

The song's lilting words about the Messiah evoked a mental image for me of a figure standing up to raging waves, taking on the burning flames, and withstanding the force of it all on my behalf as if he were a dam. As Prejean's voice faded, a tear escaped my eye. *If only that were true*, I thought. *How beautiful would that be?*

You see, when I first saw that movie, I was a Muslim. Yet the story's power to convey the gospel penetrated my otherwise closed heart. It would be a few years before I fully opened my heart to Christ, but the message of the gospel told through a movie was part of that journey. As an aside, years later I would be given the privilege of preaching at Angola Prison in Louisiana, where part of *Dead Man Walking* was filmed. At one point during my visit, Ravi and I stood in the execution chamber, somberly gazing at the table where lethal injections are administered, which was featured in the film. In that grim place, Jesus' sacrifice was made all the more palpable to me. It's amazing how God writes his poetry into our lives.

Books and movies are nothing if not drawn-out parables. The gospel story is so powerful that we seem unable to help ourselves from telling part or all of it through those modern parables. Their popularity speaks to the ongoing power of parables to speak to minds and hearts. Indeed, parables aren't always told by traveling itinerants on the hills or in the streets of Middle Eastern agrarian towns. Often they're told on silver screens or in the pages of books. Yes, parables have persisted across the centuries in different forms. But our modern parables often look like rehashes and footnotes to the timeless parables given to us by the itinerant Jewish preacher from Nazareth.

Chapter 7

THE TEMPLE AND
THE WEDDING

RAVI ZACHARIAS

In the East, no two occasions pull the family together more than visiting the temple or hosting a wedding. They are the settings in which cultural values are distilled to their essence.

Some time ago, I visited a church in Mosul, Iraq, that had been burned and desecrated by ISIS fighters. They had turned the ancient sacred space into an armed camp and vented their hatred for the Christian faith all over the walls. With tears in his eyes, the caretaker said, "I would never even read out to you the words they have written on these walls. They are horrible to read and to see."

Throughout history, invaders have known that if you really wish to humiliate your enemies, you must plunder what is most sacred to them. Of all things a culture values, nothing is worth more than its altars. People will lay down their lives to defend their sacred places. For the Jewish people, no place was dearer to them than the temple, which housed the book of the law and stored the ark of the covenant. The people's identity resided in their worship, so distinctive from all other groups. In the nation's earliest days, Abraham was called the man of the tent and the man of the altar, representing the passing brevity of life and the eternal value of worship. The tent and the altar—the family dwells in the tent; the family of God meets at the altar.

While places of worship are deemed sacred in every religion, when a nation breathes politics into its faith, the mix can be deadly—be it a mosque for the Muslims, a temple for the Hindus or Buddhists, a state-dictated Christianity, or a *gurdwara* for the Sikhs. *Gurdwara* means "the door to the guru." On October 31, 1984, Indian Prime Minister Indira Gandhi forfeited her life after Indian troops had entered a *gurdwara* in June of that year at her command because a huge cache of arms was being stored inside. At an opportune moment several months later, her closest bodyguard, a Sikh, turned his gun on her. For the Sikh community, sending the troops inside the door to the guru was the unpardonable blasphemy.

Attacks on houses of worship generate headlines around the world. A murderous onslaught at two mosques in Christchurch, New Zealand, in March 2019 left fifty-one people dead, shocking that largely peaceful nation and the world. Who can forget when a white supremacist entered a church at prayer time in Charleston, South Carolina, in June 2015 and slaughtered nine people, or when Islamist suicide bombers struck on Easter Sunday in April 2019 in Colombo, Sri Lanka, killing 253 people? People who had served me when I visited there earlier were buried under the rubble of this profane attack.

As horrifying as these incidents are, we must not overlook the unseen tragedy that happens when we, the worshipers, unwittingly profane our own places of worship even more thoroughly than any attacker from the outside.

THE TWO TEMPLES

Ancient Israel had two major temples. The first was built in the tenth century BC by King Solomon, the son of David. In 1 Kings 6:12–13, God tells Solomon, "As for this temple you are building, if you follow my decrees, observe my laws and keep all my commands and obey them, . . . I will live among the Israelites and will not abandon my people Israel."

But alas, the people, led by the priests, lost their way in worship, even as they kept up their spiritual appearances. The prophets warned them that this disconnect in their spiritual lives could cost them that which they held most dear—the temple of the Lord. They refused to listen, and in 586 BC, Nebuchadnezzar and the Babylonians sacked Jerusalem and destroyed the magnificent temple. But long before that, it had been destroyed spiritually as a place where God met his people.

Under Ezra and Nehemiah, the building of the Second Temple began around 538 BC, taking a little more than twenty years through the amazing generosity of three different foreign monarchs. Yet outside opposition to this new sacred space didn't abate. Several attempts by foreign oppressors were made to plunder Jerusalem again. Finally, under the Greek ruler Antiochus Epiphanes, a statue of the pagan god Zeus was erected in the temple, and Hellenistic priests officiated by sacrificing pigs on the altar. This profaning of the pure by the unclean sparked a successful rebellion by the outraged Jews. In 165 BC, the temple was finally rededicated to the worship of the one true God under the nation's new leader, Judas Maccabeus.

Painstakingly upgraded and replenished later by King Herod, a first-century puppet of the Roman Empire, the temple was finally destroyed in AD 70 by Roman armies. While attempts were made to rebuild the structure, it never happened. Finally, after the seventh-century conquest of Jerusalem by Islam, the Umayyad caliph Abd al-Malik began to construct a mosque on the Temple Mount.

Today the Al-Aqsa Mosque stands on this sacred site, representing perhaps the biggest threat to any future agreement regarding a peaceful coexistence between Israel and its Muslim neighbors. This is not the first or only time that a sacred site has been built on someone else's house of worship around the world. Such provocative actions provide the accelerant for religious conflagrations that can erupt at any moment.

A GREATER THAN

When Jesus walked the earth, the world was under Roman occupation and the temple still stood. In Matthew 12, Jesus' disciples began picking some grain on the Sabbath. The Sabbath was a sacred covenantal reminder to the Jew of his or her relationship with God. Its observance was the supreme expression of that bond. Now the One who claimed to be the Messiah was allowing his disciples to "violate" the rules of the Sabbath by picking grain, the Pharisees charged.

In a staggering response, Jesus refers to himself as a

"greater than"—greater than the temple (verse 6), greater than Jonah (verse 41), and greater than Solomon (verse 42). In effect, Jesus is claiming to be greater than the Sabbath itself and what it represented. These were carefully chosen categories. The temple was the Jewish people's stronghold and refuge. Solomon had built it and had spoken profound proverbs. Jonah was the messenger to the Gentile nations and had survived three days of what should have been certain death. Jesus here was saying that he was greater and had a greater message than all three.

Temples or churches are a vital part of a nation's history because they are the locus of people's ultimate allegiance. Communist nations attempt to curb or redirect worship because they wish to be the supreme authority in their subjects' lives. In Saint Petersburg, Russia, the Kazan Cathedral, where the czar prayed as Napoleon's army approached Moscow, is today a temple of atheism.

Make no mistake about it. Every nation has its temples. They either exalt the state and diminish the individual or exalt the individual, who by choice submits to the will of his Creator. The first is a superimposed value; the second is a recognition of implicit value. How did Jesus deal with this perpetual struggle within life and governance?

WHAT THE TEMPLE MEANT
AND WHAT IT BECAME

In Matthew 21:13, Jesus says, "'My house will be called a house of prayer,' but you are making it 'a den of robbers.'"

When seen from an Eastern perspective, we readily understand what he was saying. Let me illustrate.

Some years ago, I was visiting the temple of Kali in Calcutta. As you make your way toward the entrance, you must take off your shoes and walk on a dirt path. As you enter the temple area, you are part of a throng of people, all craning their necks to glimpse the fearsome statue of Kali. Amid all the noise, a man on the other side of the barricade in front of the "goddess" leans forward, his fists already full of money from worshipers who have paid to get close, ready to grab more money from other would-be pilgrims. If you park a significant amount of cash in his hand, you get the *darshan*—the presence. Our guide handed the man some money, and we got our five-second look before being pushed on by the next donor.

Then we entered an area reserved for sacrifices to Kali. A family came in, dragging a small goat by a rope. The father, dressed in spotless white, gave the goat to the priest, who positioned the animal's neck on a blood-smeared block of wood. Faster than the eye could follow, his blade dropped and the goat's head fell to the side. The man, who had brought the goat to fulfill a vow or to make a new vow, bent, dipped his finger in the freshly spilled blood, and marked his spotless white shirt and his forehead with the blood. I asked the priest, "Why was this done, and what does it mean to the man who offered this goat?" He said there is no symbolism; it is just a ritualistic act.

Change the scene to thousands of miles away and a midwestern city in the United States on a Friday night. The "faith healer" in his edifice, which has been designed to resemble Solomon's temple, draws thousands. The man, dressed in a glowing white suit, strides onto the platform. Before the healing begins, two offerings have already been taken, one to sell a message that the faith healer described as the last sermon he would ever preach. Ushers have come down the aisles and collected twenty dollars for each tape. A few minutes later, they come around again, selling "a baby picture of mine that my staff has found—a rare picture"—also for twenty dollars apiece. A regular offering is also taken. Gullibility and exploitation are hardly Eastern monopolies.

In the Old Testament, King Josiah cleansed and renovated the temple after the lost Book of the Law was rediscovered (2 Kings 22). In the New Testament, half a millennium later, Jesus cleansed the temple because it had similarly lost its mission (Matthew 21). The coming of Jesus and the reminder that he is "greater than" the temple is the supreme gift of Jesus to his followers. We do not need a specific place. We do not need to drag along a goat or a bull or buy pictures and tapes. We need a sure relationship with the One who "once for all" laid down his life for us (see Hebrews 10:10). The place is important but secondary. The person is in direct contact with the Savior.

In the Middle East today, and in Jerusalem in particular, a structure stands anywhere something significant has happened in history. Tragically, the structure often replaces the imagination of the worshiper. People can be addicted to buildings of worship and forget the Lord we worship. Our focus on buildings and particular people is a tragic loss in our understanding of how to know and love God.

The entire thrust of the Reformation was not to abolish the priesthood; it was to abolish the laity. We are all meant to be priests, having direct access to our heavenly Father. When the church becomes laden with wealth and the clergy become a necessary means to relating to God, the true treasure of the gospel is lost. This was the whole point of Jesus' simple parable in Matthew 13:45–46: "Again, the kingdom of heaven is like a merchant looking for fine pearls. When he found one of great value, he went away and sold everything he had and bought it."

Notice that the kingdom of heaven is reached in the present when God rules in your heart. It is a down payment or foreshadowing of God's ultimate rule in eternity. Time is on loan to us. Eternity is a gift. Notice also that the individual "sells," not "buys." We give up in order to be enriched. Who is it "sold" to? The Giver of life receives the one seeking life. The treasure is the intangible gift of salvation. This truth is foreign to those who run temples and "dispense" salvation to others. In Micah 6:6–8, we read:

> With what shall I come before the LORD
>   and bow down before the exalted God?
> Shall I come before him with burnt offerings,
>   with calves a year old?
> Will the LORD be pleased with thousands of rams,
>   with ten thousand rivers of olive oil?
> Shall I offer my firstborn for my transgression,
>   the fruit of my body for the sin of my soul?
> He has shown you, O mortal, what is good.
>   And what does the LORD require of you?
> To act justly and to love mercy
>   and to walk humbly with your God.

In this passage, God changes the means of access to himself from the sacrifice of objects to the surrender of the heart. Your walk with God reflects God in his mercy, and your judgments reflect God in his justice.

Justice reflects the law.

Mercy reflects grace.

Humility reflects the heart.

Within the span of the first two temples, the hundreds of laws given under Moses had now been reduced to these three. God was moving from the blood that flowed on the altars of mankind to the blood that flowed from the hill of Calvary and, ultimately, to the life of God that flows in the heart.

The hymn writer captures this:

> *Spirit of God, who dwells within my heart,*
> *wean it from sin, through all its pulses move.*
> *Stoop to my weakness, mighty as you are,*
> *and make me love you as I ought to love.*
>
> *Teach me to love you as your angels love,*
> *one holy passion filling all my frame:*
> *the fullness of the heaven-descended Dove;*
> *my heart an altar, and your love the flame.*[1]

The heart is the new altar, indestructible when surrendered to God. God's character can never be compromised. God's provision can never be bought. This gift is greater than the temple could ever offer. The East today is punctuated with temples throughout its landscape. The message of Jesus stands in stark relief.

Remembering his first Communion in 1938, Thomas Merton wrote:

Christ . . . was giving Himself for me . . .

In the Temple of God that I had just become, the One Eternal and Pure Sacrifice was offered up to the God dwelling in me: the sacrifice of God to God, and me sacrificed together with God, incorporated in His incarnation. Christ born in me, a new Bethlehem, and sacrificed in me, His new Calvary, and risen in me: offering me to the Father, in Himself, asking the Father, my Father and His, to receive me into His infinite and special love.[2]

While, as a Protestant, I would word it a little differently, at the heart of what Merton is saying is a beautiful truth. There is an aspect of Bethlehem in my spiritual journey. There is the reality of Calvary in my conversion. There is the impact of the resurrection as I live in hope. There is the temple within me in my daily worship. This is what Jesus brings to me in a comprehensive work that he accomplished on my behalf.

In war zones, the broken body becomes a limited space in which to accommodate God's indwelling presence. But worship is still real. I recall in Vietnam in the 1970s holding chapel by the bedsides of wounded soldiers. To participate in Communion there and hear the words, "This is my body broken for you," while standing by a broken body, to hear the words from Jesus, "This is the cup of the new covenant in my blood, which is poured out for you," brought home the irony of life and death in ways I had never experienced. This act of remembering the words of him who had died for the spiritually dying, though we still physically die—words immortalized by him who rose from the dead so we might rise as well—encompassed life's grimmest and most-needed truths. Combining the cleansing of the temple and our new understanding of the body as the temple is a truth that is both liberating and binding for the followers of Jesus.

As restricting as the body is, Jesus pronounced the ultimate liberation. Immediately after Jesus cleansed the temple, the onlookers demanded a sign to prove his authority to do what he had done. In a brilliant moment of translating the reality of moving the temple from the building to the body, he said, "Destroy this temple, and I will raise it again in three days" (John 2:19). Everything in that statement challenged their presuppositions. They thought he was talking about the physical temple that had taken nearly half a century to build. They had no clue that he was talking about the resurrection of his body. Just as the cleansing of the temple suddenly brought to mind for his disciples a passage from David a thousand years earlier, "Zeal for your house consumes me" (Psalm 69:9), so also only after his physical resurrection did they remember his saying, "I will raise it again in three days."

NO LAST TEMPLE

We have looked at the cleansing of the temple and the redefinition of the temple. There remains one more important link—the final temple. In Revelation 21, we see an incredible parallel and an even more incredible distinction. John is describing the new Jerusalem. God says there, "I am making everything new!" (Revelation 21:5). All the dimensions of the temple that Solomon built were carefully described (see 1 Kings 6). All the materials and the metals and the builders were given by description and by name.

Now we have the new Jerusalem. The city for which wars have been fought on earth will have a new location, with only God as owner. Worshipers from every tribe and tongue will be present. As John describes the exact dimensions of the new Jerusalem, he states, "I did not see a temple in the city, because the Lord God Almighty and the Lamb are its temple" (Revelation 21:22).

In Isaiah 49:16, the Lord says of Jerusalem, "I have engraved you on the palms of my hands; your walls are ever before me." Now in the new Jerusalem, the marks on his palms will be the marks of his crucifixion. We will no longer do battle for the cities of men. We will not need a wall. We will be inhabitants of the City of God.

Years ago, I was traveling with a Palestinian team and speaking in Jerusalem. One of the young men had lived in Jerusalem until the Six-Day War. Now he lived in Jordan as the director of the Bible Society. As we walked along the streets in the Old City, my friend and I were enjoying hummus, falafel, freshly baked pita, and the heavenly *kanafe*. My friend got rather emotional, saying, "You will never know what it means to a man like me to walk in my home city, my beloved Jerusalem. My heart beats differently."

That phrase, "my home city," hit hard. That has been the battle cry of the centuries in that part of the world. Who owns Jerusalem? Who owns the Temple Mount? To whom does the Holy City belong? This is not a battle just between the Jews and the Arabs. The Church of the Holy Sepulchre is divided into five sectors, each belonging to a different Christian sect. The leaders do not even talk to each other, so the keys to the church are held by a Muslim cleric who opens and locks it at appointed hours. Sacred sites are embattled zones where hostilities run deep.

Just as neither Hagar's son nor Sarah's son but God's Son was the ultimate sacrifice, so also in eternity, Jerusalem will not be Palestinian land or Israeli land but the City of God. There will be no zones in the Eternal City. There will be one Prophet, Priest, and King—all in one. There is only one lock—the human heart. There is only one key—the finished work of Jesus. All will bow to his authority. The new Jerusalem will have no temple. *He* will be the temple. We will be the worshipers. Our earthly temples will have been shed, and our glorified bodies will worship the glorious Lord, our temples surrendering to him.

The songwriter of old captured the imagery:

> *And once again the scene was changed,*
> *New earth there seemed to be.*
> *I saw the Holy City*
> *Beside the tideless sea.*
> *The Light of God was on its streets,*
> *The gates were open wide,*
> *And all who would might enter,*
> *And no one was denied.*
> *No need of moon or stars by night,*
> *Or sun to shine by day;*
> *It was the new Jerusalem*
> *That would not pass away.*[3]

THE WEDDING MOTIF

If the body is a temple in Christian terms, then the wedding is an altar. In Genesis, God, in his creative act, calls everything good. The first time something is not pronounced good happens when he notes that it is not good for man to be alone (Genesis 2:18). So the woman is created to walk alongside the man in a unique, consummate relationship. This relationship of mutual fulfillment is so exclusive that even God, being spirit, remains outside their physical intimacy. Such a gift to us comes with incredible possibilities and restrictions. The first wedding is officiated by God himself. He is the Minister who makes possible the two becoming one.

It is not surprising to me that in John 2:1–10, Jesus is present at a wedding. The host is running out of wine. I suspect that, like any typical wedding in the East, far more people have shown up for the reception than the host was expecting. When I was young, I attended many a wedding to which I had not been formally invited. The whole occasion is so festive that hosts expect there ought to be many more people than have received invitations.

Over the years, I have taken many friends to India. Once we were staying at a hotel where a gala wedding was taking place. The groom's father happened to meet some of my American friends in the hallway. He engaged them in a conversation before saying, "My son is getting married tonight; please come and join us for the dinner." My friends said, "Oh, we are just visiting. There are forty-five of us here in India." "Oh please," the father said. "All of you come and be my guests!" In the East, a wedding is at once as ceremonial and ritualistic as it is informal and hospitable. The invitation is wide. The commitment is exclusive. Nothing is more important in a family's life than a wedding.

It is beautiful simply to see Jesus at a wedding. But then an incredible conversation takes place. His mother asks him to intervene. Typical mother. "They have no more wine," she says (verse 3). Like a little boy asked by his parents to sing at a birthday party, Jesus says, in effect, "Why are you dragging me into this? This is not my time!" (verse 4, paraphrased). A typical son. But something extraordinary happens. "Do whatever he tells you," she commands the servants (verse 5). Jesus proceeds to give the servants their instructions.

No Easterner reading this story can feel anything but intrigue. We love weddings and fear running out of food. So we spend big on weddings in a game of one-upmanship. We feast at weddings, and, yes, many go broke at weddings. Jesus did his first miracle at a wedding, turning the water into wine. The family must have had a post-wedding discussion on inviting Mary to all future family events!

The fact that Jesus was seen at this wedding was completely ordinary. But there is another event for which the motif of a wedding is extraordinary. Jesus says that the culmination of this earthly existence will be a wedding (Matthew 22:1–14). He will come as the bridegroom, and the church is his bride (Matthew 25:1–12). Jesus borrows from daily life in the East to illustrate the final scene for humanity.

In the East, we talk of arranged marriages. In the West, we talk of romance and marriage. Each has its weaknesses; each has its strengths. At the end of history as we know it, God in an amazing way will bring together the strengths of both, in a day that has long been seen by God before it has come to be. He has arranged the final moment.

THE ONLY CONSUMMATE LOVE

C. S. Lewis talks of the four loves: God's love, protective love, friendship love, and romantic love.[4] Marriage is the only love that binds all four in one. When Jesus returns, the replacement of the physical by the spiritual makes the consummate spiritual experience possible. That which God excluded himself from—the physical—he now transcends by the spiritual.

In Matthew 22:1–14, Jesus tells a parable of a wedding banquet. The Sadducees invoke the Old Testament's Levirate marriage law (Matthew 22:24–28; see Deuteronomy 25:5–10; Ruth 1), which gives a widow the privilege or responsibility to marry the brother of her deceased husband. The Sadducees, who do not believe in a resurrection of the dead, cunningly try to trip up Jesus with a trick question. They ask him what will happen in the resurrection to the widow if there is a resurrection and she has followed the law and married her deceased husband's seven brothers in turn. "Whose wife will she be?" (verse 28).

Can't you just see them rehearsing that question with back-slapping hilarity in preparing to trip up Jesus? Jesus, however, silences them by affirming that there is no marriage in heaven. What? No temple? No marriage? Marriage is a physical union that symbolizes the ultimate spiritual union. Marriage is a shadow of the ultimate reality of our union with Jesus. When the real has come, the shadow is no longer needed. Just as there will be no physical temple, there will be no physical consummation.

The apostle Paul uses this metaphor in Ephesians 5:25: "Husbands, love your wives, just as Christ loved the church and gave himself up for her." In the final book of the Bible, John picks up this theme again. In Revelation 19:7–9, he writes, "Let us rejoice and be glad and give him glory! For the wedding of the Lamb has come, and his bride has made herself ready. Fine linen, bright and clean, was given her to wear . . . Then the angel said to me, 'Write this: Blessed are those who are invited to the wedding supper of the Lamb!' And he added, 'These are the true words of God.'"

Christ the bridegroom. The church the bride. In the very next section in Revelation, the groom is described as coming on a white horse (19:11). This is exactly how every groom comes to his bride in Indian weddings. She is adorned and veiled. He comes as the "victor," the one who has won the right to love her, with playing bands and dancing guests following behind. It is a day to celebrate. The parables of the wedding and the teaching of Jesus on marriage are so powerful and eternal. As the designer of marriage, he gives us the true definition of marriage. His teaching is the starting point and the ending point.

While Jesus gives us the ideal for marriage, he is also gracious to those who have faltered. During his conversation with the woman at the well, he asked her to call her husband. That was an incredible ask, but he had a reason. She candidly replied, "I have no husband" (John 4:17). When she acknowledged this, he surprised her further by saying that, indeed, not only did he know that she did not have a husband;

her present arrangement was with her sixth partner. "The man you now have is not your husband" (verse 18). He knew who she was and what her heartaches were. Jesus ever places before us the ideal and shows us the cost of failure, but he still reaches out to us for a new start. None of this is traditionally present in Eastern culture. A woman such as the woman at the well would be branded either as lewd, stupid, or a total failure.

Before I wrote the book *Has Christianity Failed You?*[5] we interviewed people about why they had walked away from the church. Their number was large. I cannot forget a woman who said she left her church because her marriage had failed and the church had never forgiven her. It was a sad story. While it is true that one cannot celebrate failure, it is also true that the ones who have faltered know best what it means. They know the pain of their failure. They know the anguish of a breakup, the cost of an amputated relationship. They are the first to admit failure. They don't need to be reminded. Adding insult to injury injures the spirit more than the body. This is where, when sin is great, the grace of God is greater.

But Jesus has something else to say to the East and the West when it comes to the family. The East prides itself on the prominence it gives to the family and to parents, who are a vital part of any decision because they brought us into the world. Indeed, the Bible, which originates from the East, tells us to honor our father and our mother (Exodus 20:12). But honoring your parents should not give them the right of ownership, and that is hard for an Easterner to understand.

Once I was invited to dinner in an Iranian home. My friend's father, who was in his eighties, was theologically dogmatic. After the meal he started quizzing me with deep, penetrating challenges, and I was somewhat taken aback. My friend, the host, did something very difficult, especially in an Eastern family. He said, "Papa! Ravi is my guest. I want you to respect that and not make this evening an examination of his theology." There was silence around the table. My friend's father knew a line had been drawn, and it must have been hard to accept with grace. But he did.

How difficult it is for parents to respect the sovereign responsibility of their children that comes with establishing a new home! This remains a soul-struggle in the East, as parental control has to be surrendered to the new couple, who now must exercise their own maturity and responsibility. Parents must love, advise, and counsel, yes—but control, no! There comes a time when the new relationship has priority over the old. This is painful, but so is birth itself. The bride and groom set up a new home to perpetuate the inherited legacy.

Then there is the issue of love. The West prides itself on love *before* marriage, while the East prides itself on love *after* marriage. Neither extreme has it right. Love may precede the union, but love must also follow the ceremony. What precedes gives one the privilege of choice. What follows is a death to selfish pursuits. We are made in the image of God. Our bodies are the temples of God. The union between two people is the mystical embrace of two temples housing the One who instituted marriage.

When a man and a woman marry, they both become the bride for the supreme Bridegroom who comes for us. When that happens, there will be no more temple, because we lay our all at his feet. He is the temple; we are the worshipers. The temple and the wedding bridge the two great institutions

God had in mind from the beginning—the immediate family and the spiritual family. Both are connected and are to be perpetuated.

At every Christian Indian wedding, this famous hymn is sung:

The voice that breathed o'er Eden,
That earliest wedding day,
The primal marriage blessing,
It hath not passed away.

Still in the pure espousal
Of Christian man and maid
The Triune God is with us,
The threefold grace is said.

For dower of blessèd children,
For love and faith's sweet sake,
For high mysterious union
Which naught on earth may break.

Be present, loving Father,
To give away this bride
As thou gav'st Eve to Adam,
Out of his own pierced side:

Be present, Son of Mary,
To join their loving hands
As thou didst bind two natures
In Thine eternal bands.

Be present, Holiest Spirit,
To bless them as they kneel,
As Thou for Christ, the Bridegroom,
The Heavenly Spouse dost seal.

O spread Thy pure Wing o'er them,
Let no ill power find place
When onward to Thine Altar
The hallow'd path they trace.

To cast their crowns before Thee
In humble sacrifice,
Till to the home of gladness
With Christ's own Bride they rise.[6]

The temple and the wedding constitute the two earthly representations of our worship and communion with God. The beautiful and unique teaching of Jesus brings them together in a way that bridges East and West.

Chapter 8

THE TEMPTATION AND THE TRANSFIGURATION

Ravi Zacharias

Life at its most barren and life at the mountaintop. Two important episodes in the life of Jesus, the temptation and the transfiguration, take place in contrasting settings but teach similar truths. Jesus shows us what real temptation is and what our real mission in life must be. These stories are deeply connected.

THE TEMPTATION AS REAL

Contrary to others who claimed divine or prophetic status, Jesus knew his identity and his mission. This is not so, for example, in Muhammad's life. We are told in Islamic teaching that his wife encouraged him to go back and seek the vision; perhaps the angel was trying to tell him something.

How does one explain that the "greatest" prophet needed an ordinary person to explain to him who he was? Muhammad was in his midtwenties. Was his mission so unclear that he needed someone else, including his wife and uncle, to set that calling before him?

In complete contrast, at the wedding in Cana, Jesus responds to his mother by saying that the time had not yet come to disclose his identity (John 2:4). He knew his purpose and the timeline for his disclosure. Self-awareness of his divine calling was present from the start. To honor the law, Jesus chose to be baptized and filled with the Holy Spirit. Jesus' very life would fulfill the law and show us something even greater. After his baptism and before the beginning of his public ministry, Jesus further identified with humanity in what we call the temptation. No human eye saw this episode. The Lord was alone, ravaged by the elements on the outside and hunger on the inside. He was fair game for the tempter.

The question is often asked, "Was Jesus not able to sin or was he able not to sin?" Phrasing the question in that way, we miss what is actually happening. He was tempted, as are we, *within the context of who he was.* He was the Son of God, the One sent by the Father to save the world from sin. Satan stayed within those boundaries.

Jesus cautioned us against lust, greed, and pride. In his context, the temptations would be the lust of power, the greed of recognition, and the pride of being supreme. To tempt him outside of who he was would be like tempting a billionaire with five dollars. That would not be a struggle for a wealthy man. But if you tempted a major stockholder with the power to control the stock market, there would indeed be a struggle.

That is why every temptation thrown at Jesus begins with "if you are the Son of God," either stated or implied.

We are all tempted within our own contexts. We all struggle. I remember a congressman from our city who was offered a large sum of money for certain understood favors. He took the money. Days later, he felt guilty and tried to return the money, but it was too late. The whole thing had been a setup, and he had been caught on camera. Many temptations have those ingredients—the setup, a momentary yielding, disappointment, guilt, and an attempt to hide or redeem oneself, followed by the harshness of human judgment.

We see the beginning of a setup when Jesus is in the desert. However, both the struggle with evil and the appearance of evil are eliminated by his response. He did not err and then need to seek to make amends. How unlike us!

Some years ago, I read an article on ethics in an airline magazine that illustrated the author's perspective with an apocryphal story about a man on a flight who propositioned the woman sitting next to him for one million dollars. At first, she flatly turned him down, but as the flight progressed and their conversation continued, she eventually changed her mind.

Minutes before they landed, he turned to her and said, "I'm sorry to say this, but I simply don't have a million dollars. Would you consider the same proposal for ten dollars?"

In utter disgust, she said to him, "What do you think I am?"

He paused and said, "We have already established that; we are now just haggling over the price."

In our hearts, life is a matter of haggling over the price

for who we really are. The article's author concluded we all have a price and if it is met, each of us will sell out. We can debate that ad nauseam, but we do know this: in our hearts we all falter.

What do we feel when we have violated what we know is good? The remorse that comes is not merely regret; it is a guilt that is felt because an objective moral law has been violated. The French mystic Michel Quoist writes a powerful prayer titled "I Have Fallen":

> *I have fallen, Lord,*
> *Once more.*
> *I can't go on, I'll never succeed.*
> *I am ashamed, I don't dare look at you.*
> *And yet I struggled, Lord, for I knew you were right*
> *near me, bending over me, watching.*
> *But temptation blew like a hurricane*
> *And instead of looking at you I turned my head away.*
> *I stepped aside*
> *While you stood, silent and sorrowful,*
> *Like the spurned fiancé who sees his loved one carried*
> *away by the enemy.*[1]

I'm afraid these sorrowful words convey a scene with which we are all too familiar. We had a choice. We made the wrong choice. We wish to take it back. But it's too late. There is no recourse but to mourn the loss.

Jesus, however, had no price. We see who he was in the way he responded. We see no remorse, which proved his power. Out of that power he offers us his grace and forgiveness.

Let us examine his three temptations more closely to better see his identity and power from an Eastern perspective.[2]

MATERIAL SEDUCTION

The first temptation was, "If you are the Son of God, tell these stones to become bread" (Matthew 4:3). Talk about a taunt! For Jesus, this was a true temptation to do something he knew he had the power to do. Succumbing to it would have served two purposes: (1) He was hungry and could have appeased his hunger, and (2) the act could have attracted a following for his mission.

But this would have meant obeying the whim of the one who wished to destroy him, changing his faith into pragmatism. Certainly, if he could turn water into wine, he could have turned stones into bread. And the thought of doing so was a real temptation because the thought of bread probably tormented him in his need. "You need it; the world needs it. Do it!" But meeting the immediacy of his need could have cost him the eternality of his mission. The tempter was trying to seduce Jesus into providing the kind of proof that would gain him a following for all the wrong reasons, the very opposite of faith. This temptation lurks within the human heart to this day: Why does Jesus not prove himself to us in more spectacular or commanding ways?

Jesus answered the temptation with the eternal word: "Man shall not live on bread alone, but on every word that comes from the mouth of God." The key words here are *live* and *bread alone*.

What does it mean to live? I have been told that on flights to Las Vegas people are generally full of hilarity and hope but that flights out are filled with somber passengers with disappointment writ large on their faces. When we gamble with life, our hopes for winning are fraught with pain and disappointment. Even if we win the prize, it is never enough, and the joy doesn't last.

"Bread alone" is wrongheaded! Some years ago, a businessman who took his life in Las Vegas left a note: "Here there are no answers." He didn't say whether he had won or lost, but he did say there were *no answers* to be found in this way of living. What were his unanswered questions? I suspect they had to do with the kind of bread that would have satisfied him.

The qualifier "alone" reminds us that for Jesus, truth for the soul and sustenance for the body are applied by truth for the body and sustenance for the soul. Had Jesus said, "Man shall not live on bread," he would have spoken a platitude that was open to attack. He fed the masses. He went fishing with fishermen. Even after his resurrection, he asked for food. Jesus was not against bread.

But as he broke bread with his disciples, the Lord bridged the physical with the spiritual. The act of taking Holy Communion, which Jesus initiated, even includes the sensation of taste. Yet Jesus, in effect, defined for us what it means to live. It is the life of the soul.

In this temptation we also see the difference between faith and reason. Reason says that if we satisfy our material needs, faith necessarily follows. Faith says that although our material needs are important, true faith will never be born in us if the heart has been won by material gain alone. What people are won *with* is often what they are won *to*. Jesus denies either extreme—a focus on material gain and a focus on no material gain—by adding the qualifier "alone." Faith and reason are forever in an interplay.

I have often said that God has put enough into this world to make faith in him most reasonable, but he has left enough out to make it impossible to live by reason alone. The skeptic often caricatures the Christian faith as credulity. That is not how the Bible sees it. Real faith is based on reason and what we know to be true. It helps carry us over the chasms of our doubt when not every question is answered. Our faith is in the One whom we know offers us eternal life. He demonstrated that with enough reason, we may trust him for what we don't know.

Although this temptation on the surface appears to be material, at its core it is *intellectual*. Can't God do more to show me his material power so I will be intellectually justified in following him? Faith cannot be *totally* blind, we say. But Jesus remarkably shows us that there is more to the walk of faith than an ever-present demand for additional proof. Satan failed in his bid to divide what God had joined together. Faith requires us to see beyond the immediate.

POWER CORRUPTS

The second temptation was a lust for power and control—even to the point of demanding the submission of the Father to Jesus' will, as if to tempt Jesus to make a demand of the Father: "I am going to jump. You prove yourself by protecting me from injury." The first temptation was to compel a demonstration of Jesus' power so that the world would believe. The second temptation was to compel the Father to prove himself. At its heart is the same temptation—to control God according to your own wishes and timetable. At its core, it is a *quest for power*. The world of politics is plagued with this malady at the cost of millions of lives.

Jesus renounced his right to draw from God's power at will because he was committed to his mission to obey his Father and lay down his life for us. Power was legitimately his, but Satan offered it to him illegitimately. For our sakes, Jesus renounced it. In an Eastern setting, where a show of power is crucial for success, Jesus' response is a staggering surprise. True power as he modeled it consisted not in doing what he had the *power* to do but in choosing to do what he *ought* to do.

Jesus couldn't be drawn into politics, because by doing so, his message would be polluted by the politically driven. He couldn't be seduced by the interests of the moment, because his mission was eternal. He couldn't be goaded into looking good in the eyes of others, because his mission was to *do* good. Jesus laid aside his rights in order to do what was right. He had a power greater than any politician, but he refused to be possessed by it so that he could meet our need—the reason he had come. Too often we live under the illusion that our answers can be found in politics.

One night when I was a young lad, my father, in a fit of rage, literally threw the family out of the house. My mother, with the five of us children, sat under a stairwell situated between four flats. It was a cold night, and she unwrapped half of her sari to provide us with our only shelter. That night, my father thought he had the power to humiliate us. That night, the humble spirit of my mother won me over forever.

Later, my mother was given an opportunity to go to the United Kingdom to advance her studies and seal a powerful career. She turned down the opportunity because she knew her five children needed her at home. Years later, both my parents gave their lives to the Lord. A few more years went by before we lost my mother when she was in her fifties. My dad stood by her coffin, stroking her head and muttering words of apology and remorse for the years of sorrow he had inflicted on her.

The cross had won! Well before my mom passed, my dad had become a changed man. He had been brought from an addiction to power to the "expulsive power of a new affection," as Thomas Chalmers puts it in his famous sermon—the power of the cross of Jesus Christ.[3]

Resisting the temptation to draw from the power of his Father in order to win a small battle with the tempter, Jesus went the distance to win the greater battle for humanity. The cross was in his sight even before the throne.

Ironically, I am writing these words in a part of the world where ironfisted dictators have crushed millions of lives over the decades, all in a thirst for power. I fear that we are slowly following the same path in the West as well. The response of Jesus to the temptation to misuse the power available to him is a breath of fresh air from another realm.

WANTING PLEASURE, KILLING WORSHIP

In the final temptation, Satan offered Jesus "all the kingdoms of the world and their splendor" (Matthew 4:8). In return, all Jesus had to do was worship him. Now it was Satan who sought complete power, attempting to shift the Lord's focus from the cost of worshiping him to the benefit he offered: "All this I will give you" (verse 9). This temptation to ownership is an offer to the eyes for ownership of the heart. If the eyes ruled, the heart would be lost.

As a young teen, I had never read a narrative like Jesus' temptation that was so relevant and yet so real. Jesus' response to this final offer went beyond the merely momentarily relevant to a timeless reality. While Jesus did not feel exactly the same things we do under temptation, this does not mean his experience was irrelevant and that he could not relate to us. To think that misses what lies at the heart of temptation. Sensuality is not really the temptation here. Instead, as with all temptations, it is the immediate versus the eternal. It is ultimate purpose sold at the altar of pragmatism.

To misunderstand this particular test of power is to confuse what is essentially powerful and what is merely a surface flex of the muscles. To think of bread as "bread alone" is to deny oneself the greater treasure of what life is all about. The temptation episode is the entire gospel in a few verses. The cross of Jesus is indispensable and is often seductively obscured by the enemy of our souls. His desire to own our hearts clouds our need to surrender to the One who made us. It obscures the purpose God desires for each of us.

Purpose is the one thing I did not have before Jesus. Yes, I had tiny little meanings but no ultimate meaning. This narrative, however, seals it for me. Satan desires our worship. To get it, he seduces us from the worship of the living God who has made us for himself. Jesus rebuked Satan and told him we were designed to worship only the Lord our God and serve him only. Worship has to be pure if it is to be meaningful.

Arthur Leonard Griffith shows us the subtle nature of this temptation in *God's Time and Ours*:

> Satan tempts us at the point of our physical needs, not that we might gratify them to excess, but that we might think of nothing else, and satisfy them at the expense of our usefulness in the world.
>
> Satan tempts us at the point of our ambitions, not that we might engage in positive evil, but that we might simply accept the fact of evil, learn to live with it, come to terms with it, and maintain a quiet reverence in the presence of it.
>
> Satan tempts us at the point of our religion, not that we might disbelieve in God, but that we might demand certainty, that type of certainty of God that leaves nothing to faith, nothing to God himself.[4]

Jesus' response to this third temptation was straightforward. Only one is worthy of worship, he said. The kingship of Jesus is manifested in the surrender of a person's heart. Jesus resisted the allurement of the *intellect* in the first temptation, the allurement of the *will* in the second, and the allurement of the *imagination* in the third. In so doing, he overcame the penalty brought about by the first Adam in the Garden of Eden, who chose instead to play God. Jesus, in the desert, chose to let God be God.

THE TRANSFIGURATION:
A MOUNTAINTOP VIEW

From the desert we turn our attention to the mountain, from the experience of gnawing hunger to spectacular affirmation.[5] The desert saved the road to the cross and made it possible. The mountain gave a glimpse of heaven. It is only because of the first that the second is possible.

In Matthew 16:17–19, Jesus affirmed the apostle Peter because he had recognized who Jesus was in his being. But Peter was also seriously chastised for failing to understand Jesus' mission (verse 23). The Son of God—yes; the cross—no. That was Peter, even at his best. At the end of the chapter, we have a perplexing statement when Jesus says, "Truly I tell you, some who are standing here will not taste death before they see the Son of Man coming in his kingdom" (verse 28).

The next chapter, Matthew 17, gives a foretaste of what Jesus meant. Jesus takes Peter, James, and John to a high mountain. They have no clue what they are about to witness. The Bible says "he was transfigured before them. His face shone like the sun, and his clothes became as white as the light. Just then there appeared before them Moses and Elijah, talking with Jesus" (verses 2–3).

Their first reaction was shock. These three young Jewish men would have considered Moses and Elijah to be two of the greatest prophets. One had led the people to the Promised Land; the other had challenged the worship of Baal and won. One dealt with false monarchs, the other with false prophets. And both Moses and Elijah shared one thing in common—God himself had been their undertaker. Neither of them has a known burial site. Moses, who had been deprived of seeing the Promised Land because of his shortcomings, finally did set his foot in the Promised Land at the transfiguration. I wonder what he and Elijah were talking about with Jesus. Could Moses have been saying, "Thank you, Lord! I wanted so much to be here"?

If Peter knew the Scriptures, he must have drawn courage. He too would falter, and he too would be forgiven. So overpowering was this experience that Peter did not want to leave that place. Peter the fisherman was willing to become Peter the builder. "If you wish," he says to Jesus, "I will put up three shelters—one for you, one for Moses and one for Elijah" (verse 4). Just imagine that offer. Peter is so much a man of the hour that he forgets eternity. "This is amazing!" he's saying. "Let's stay here. Make this your residence. We will build it." That's the wish, isn't it?

While Peter was waxing eloquent about his plans, a voice came from the heavens: "This is my Son, whom I love; with him I am well pleased. Listen to him!" (verse 5)—essentially, "Instead of talking, listen!" The disciples now had a glimpse of what had happened at Jesus' baptism at the dawn of his ministry. The affirmation of the Father's love and good pleasure is stated again, toward the sunset hours of Jesus' life.

When God spoke, the three disciples fell facedown. Jesus, however, comforted them and told them they had no reason to fear. When they opened their eyes, they were alone with him. No crowd. No Moses and Elijah. Jesus reminded them that there was work to be done and a mission to be finished.

The Mount of Transfiguration would lead to the Hill of Crucifixion. Peter had already reacted with dismay at the prospect of the cross, but now as Jesus was headed there following the transfiguration, Peter needed this spectacular revelation. Even as he had followed Jesus up the mountain, not knowing what awaited, neither did he know now that ultimately he would be taken to a place of his own crucifixion. I want to highlight two passages from Peter's epistles, written after the death of Jesus and before Peter's own martyrdom.

In 2 Peter 1:16–21, the apostle states the following, clearly harking back to this experience:

> For we did not follow cleverly devised stories when we told you about the coming of our Lord Jesus Christ in power, but we were eyewitnesses of his majesty. He received honor and glory from God the Father when the voice came to him from the Majestic Glory, saying, 'This is my Son, whom I love; with him I am well pleased.' We ourselves heard this voice that came from heaven when we were with him on the sacred mountain.
>
> We also have the prophetic message as something completely reliable, and you will do well to pay attention to it, as to a light shining in a dark place, until the day dawns and the morning star rises in your hearts. Above all, you must understand that no prophecy of Scripture came about by the prophet's own interpretation of things. For prophecy never had its origin in the human will, but prophets, though human, spoke from God as they were carried along by the Holy Spirit.

So much is said in these few verses. They speak to the fulfillment of Jesus' words, "Some who are standing here will not taste death before they see the Son of Man coming in his kingdom" (Matthew 16:28). The words *see* and *coming* in this passage foreshadow the ultimate return of Jesus. Peter uses similar phrasing: "coming of our Lord Jesus Christ," "eyewitnesses," and "he received glory and honor."

Peter reminds us here of some easily forgotten truths: (1) No experience, however thrilling, has the lasting value that the written Word does; (2) the Scriptures were not invented by human beings—God spoke; and (3) the Trinity is involved in the writing of the Scriptures—they are revealed by the Father, as the biblical authors who wrote them were empowered by the Holy Spirit, to tell the story of the Son's coming and sacrifice.

There is a connection to the temptation here. One cannot continually bask in the glow of an experience—there is work to be done. One needs the Word of God to thwart any seduction; Jesus quoted Scripture when he was tempted. Peter, meanwhile, reminds us that we have the word of the prophets as "something completely reliable"—more certain than our experiences, as wonderful and edifying as those experiences may be. Having and knowing the Word is even above witnessing the transfiguration. As far as evidence is concerned, every experience, however thrilling, has a shelf life. We cannot go to the Mount of Transfiguration every day. It is an attestation, but it cannot provide enduring energy for the soul. Only the completely reliable Word has that power.

In the second passage (1 Peter 3:15–16), this same Peter reminds me of and defines my calling to be a Christian apologist. It is a role we all must play at some time.

But in your hearts revere Christ as Lord. Always be prepared to give an answer to everyone who asks you to give the reason for the hope that you have. But do this with gentleness and respect, keeping a clear conscience, so that those who speak maliciously against your good behavior in Christ may be ashamed of their slander.

Just imagine an ordinary fisherman describing what it means to be a good apologist. It would have been more expected from men like Paul or Apollos or even Luke, who makes such a strong case for the Jesus of history. But for an ordinary man from the workaday world to become the inspiration for Christian apologetics tells us so much about the God whom we serve.

"In your hearts revere Christ as Lord," Peter says—the spiritual depth of the apologist; "always be prepared to give an answer"—the preparation of the heart and mind of the apologist; "to everyone who asks"—the breadth necessary for the apologist; "do this with gentleness and respect"— the demeanor of the apologist; "so that those who speak maliciously . . . may be ashamed of their slander"—the character of the apologist. All these words from one who saw the transfigured body of our Lord.

Once again, we can see a connection between the temptation and the transfiguration.

- The temptation was between Jesus alone and the enemy; after his victory, angels came and attended him.
- The transfiguration Jesus shared with his three best friends; here the greatest voice attested to him.

- After the temptation, Jesus began his ministry; after the transfiguration, the disciples were prepared for their ministry.
- John the Baptist had baptized Jesus before he went into the desert temptation; in the mountain setting of the transfiguration, Jesus let his disciples know that John the Baptist was the foretold forerunner to the coming of Messiah.

Connecting dots such as these are very important to the Eastern mind.

THE EASTERN CONNECTION: COSMIC AND INDIVIDUAL

Connecting the dots in words and symbols is a hallmark of Eastern cultures. They are full of festivals and remembrances that retrace their histories and stories. Such remembrance is woven into the fabric of the Bible too. Just before his death, Joshua recalls for the people the story of their deliverance from Egypt (Joshua 24:1–28). In the New Testament, just before Stephen is stoned to death, he traces God's dealings with the people from the time of Abraham to the present, culminating with the killing of Jesus (Acts 7:1–53). Speaking on Mars Hill, Paul goes all the way back to creation in telling the story of God's relationship with humanity (Acts 17:22–31).

One of the Bible's greatest chapters in this regard is Luke 24, which relates the postresurrection appearance of Jesus to the disciples on the Emmaus road. They don't know who

Jesus is as he joins them, even as he traces all of biblical history for them. Quite overwhelmed with how he connects the dots, they invite the Lord to stay for dinner, where he continues his discourse while they listen with rapt attention. When Jesus finally breaks a piece of bread in their presence, Luke says that "their eyes were opened" (verse 31); they remembered who had done this in the same way before and realized who he was. They knew he was Jesus, and they finally understood that he had conquered the grave.

The Bible is not an emotive record. It is a studied story with every detail being important. It connects the dots both of prophecy and of its message. It tells of the past, the present, and the future. That is why even the keeping of the Lord's Supper is a transcending of time. "For whenever you eat this bread and drink this cup [in the present], you proclaim the Lord's death [in the past] until he comes [in the future]" (1 Corinthians 11:26).

The amazing thing is not just that Jesus connects the dots in history, but that he reminds us of his sovereign direction in our lives. I have no doubt that when we come into his presence at the end of our earthly lives, our first realization will be that everything in our past happened for a reason.

At my conversion, my mother read to me these words of Jesus: "Because I live, you also will live" (John 14:19). That verse lit up my soul, showing me what I was really longing for and needing from the Lord. That was in 1963. In 1974, when my mother died, my father asked me what verse we should put on her gravestone. I suggested John 14:19, and those words were inscribed on the stone.

During the early 1990s, my wife and I were in Delhi

and decided to visit my grandmother's grave. She had died in 1955, and it was no small feat to find the plot number. We discovered that the gravestone had sunk into the ground by at least a foot. After some effort, we got the gardener to dig out the detritus that had piled up on the plot over almost forty years. As he dug away the rubble, one spadeful at a time, we wondered whether we were really at the right spot. Then he hit stone. We knew it was a gravestone.

Shovel by shovel, the dirt was lifted, and the stone was gradually revealed. All of a sudden, my grandmother's name became visible, and my wife clutched my arm. There it was— her name, the date of her death, and then the same verse etched on my heart and on my mother's grave: "Jesus said, 'Because I live, you also will live.'" For me, the dots were connected—1955 . . . 1963 . . . 1974 . . . the 1990s . . . and on into the future.

When I trace the temptation and the transfiguration in the life of Jesus, I am profoundly moved. He identified with us in our struggles. But he was from eternity in the bosom of his Father. That glowing white radiance that shone on him and from within him at his transfiguration reminds us that the light of heaven at present is too blinding for us to fully see and not be smitten. But it is the radiance we will ultimately see when our beings are in their eternal state. The songwriter says:

> To God be the glory—great things He hath done!
> So loved He the world that He gave us His Son,
> Who yielded His life an atonement for sin,
> And opened the lifegate that all may go in.

Great things He hath taught us, great things He hath done,
And great our rejoicing through Jesus the Son;
But purer and higher and greater will be
Our wonder, our transport, when Jesus we see.[6]

These words were written by Fanny Crosby, who was blind. She knew what it would mean to finally see. It ultimately means seeing who Jesus is and why he is the Savior of the world.

As I look at Jesus, I see him as thoroughly Eastern. But as I read his message, I see the great impact he has had on the West. Unfortunately, many in the West have changed his transcultural message into a Westernized product, losing the Eastern perspective. We in the West have wedded the philosophies of postmodernism and Eastern mysticism, neither of which has truth as its foundation stone. If only we understood how Eastern is Jesus' touch, yet how global is his reach, we would realize that the Son truly rises in the East but casts his light on the West. His truth knows no boundaries.

People often ask me where the West is headed. I think of the words of Alexander Pope, bemoaning the loss of our moral framework.

Religion blushing veils her sacred fires,
And unawares Morality expires.
Nor public Flame, nor private, dares to shine;
Nor human Spark is left, nor Glimpse divine!
Lo! thy dread Empire, Chaos! is restor'd;
Light dies before thy uncreating word:
Thy hand, great Anarch! lets the curtain fall;
And universal Darkness buries All.[7]

We are reminded at every dawn and dusk that a new day is dawning somewhere, even as dusk descends in another part of the world. So it is with the work of God in the souls of people in various cultures. Arthur Hugh Clough says it so well:

> For while the tired waves, vainly breaking,
> Seem here no painful inch to gain,
> Far back, through creeks and inlets making,
> Comes silent, flooding in the main.
>
> And not by eastern windows only,
> When daylight comes, comes in the light,
> In front, the sun climbs slow, how slowly,
> But westward, look, the land is bright.[8]

Historically, the gospel came from the East to the West and traveled back again to the East. Now, as many from the East move West, they bring with them the message that transformed their hearts through Jesus Christ of Nazareth. May this timeless message of Jesus shine its light here, and around the world, once more. His story is full of surprises. It is not over yet. Whoever has ears, let them hear.

Chapter 9

WHY SHOULD WESTERNERS CARE HOW EASTERNERS SEE JESUS?

ABDU MURRAY

I t was quite a marvel to behold. Frantic splashing sounds had caught my attention as I rested my sore feet during a long and hot mountain hike. Curious, I ventured up the stream that hurried down from melting snowcaps to the valley below. I looked down to find about a dozen frenzied salmon spawning under a half-melted ice shelf that jutted out over the stream.

The salmon had swum against the strong current up the mountain to arrive at that spot. The fact that I needed to catch my breath on my uphill climb made the salmon's endurance all the more impressive. That salmon swim upstream to spawn is common knowledge. It's one thing to hear or read about the phenomenon; it's quite another to behold it with your own eyes.

The currents of our cultural narratives flow just as strongly—perhaps more strongly—than the mountain stream those salmon swam against. Any attempt to swim against the cultural stream requires even more strength and endurance. The narrative current flowing through Western culture today is that Christianity is an imperialistic religion devised by white males to dominate and control dark-skinned people. Put another way more applicable to the theme of this book, Christianity is characterized as a Western religious tool used to oppress and suppress Easterners.

Similarly, there is a strong current that views Christianity as a tool of male domination. In a time when social justice captures society's focus and the issues of racism, sexism, and oppression make headlines in both the West and the East, it seems impossible to swim against that narrative current. It can be done, but only when we have a fresh perspective of Christianity—or rather a *refreshed* perspective. We need to recapture the Easternness of Christianity. We need to get a fresh look at Jesus from the East.

Indeed, that's why it's so important for Westerners to care about how Easterners actually see Jesus and hear his gospel. The fact that Jesus was Middle Eastern and taught and acted within the communal honor-shame framework shows that Christianity is not a Western religion. Yet Jesus opposed the commonplace ethnic, racial, and gender discrimination of his day, the very issues that Westerners still struggle to solve. Ironically, the Christian gospel has much to offer in addressing the very problems it's often blamed for. This alone is reason enough for Westerners to behold the Eastern Jesus afresh.

Having been a Muslim most of my life, I now have been a Christian for nearly two decades, following a lengthy (and emotionally painful) exploration of the gospel's credibility. My Middle Eastern heritage and Western surroundings balanced my search. What struck me during that exploration—and still strikes me—is Christianity's *Eastern* and *Middle Easternness*. On every page of both the Old and New Testaments, I hear the Levantine accents of those speaking.

As a Middle Easterner, every time I read Bible stories, a smile crawls across my face, because its aphorisms sound so much like those my relatives use. I can almost smell the spices of dishes I came to love as a child. My heart warms at the examples of hospitality. After all, Jesus and his disciples were not sharing apple pies, French fries, or hot dogs as they ministered to those around them. The Bible's Eastern tang is so pungent that one wonders how it has come to be viewed as a Western, white religion.

Reading the Bible through my Western lenses, I see also how Jesus appeals to Western minds. If the East is based on *communal conformity*, the West is based on *individualism* and *countercultural nonconformity*. Having been raised in the West, I can see just how countercultural Jesus was, despite his Easternness. While he naturally expressed the communal nature of the Middle East, Jesus often extolled the virtues of the individualism that Westerners have come to value so much. In a patriarchal and often misogynistic society, Jesus shocked those around him by lifting women to their rightful status as equals. He bucked the ethnocentrism of his day as well. Jesus—the Middle Easterner—swam against his cultural current.

Somehow all of that had escaped my attention until I decided to examine the Bible seriously. When I was a Muslim, I thought that the Bible whitewashed Jesus, while the Qur'an depicted his Middle Eastern quality. When I read the Bible to really explore it, however, I discovered the opposite. The biblical Jesus is a fully fleshed-out person, steeped in Middle Eastern qualities, whereas in the Qur'an he is somewhat shallowly portrayed.

What's more striking is that somehow Jesus' olive oil quality had escaped the attention of Christians who tried to share the gospel with me. That's the power of today's narrative currents that tell us that Christianity is a white, male religion. "Familiarity," as the saying goes, "breeds contempt." And in the West, familiarity and complacency have diluted the gospel's Eastern tang. The curry and cumin of the gospel's originality has been replaced with the ketchup and mayo of complacency, angst, guilt, and virtue signaling.

This is another important reason why Westerners should care how Eastern Jesus is. As the West becomes more and more concerned with whether nonwhites and women are being oppressed, we would do well to recapture the reality that nonwhites were Christianity's original champions and martyrs. So much blame for cultural ills has been laid at Christianity's feet that it's time to reassess the positive impact Jesus can have today.

An encounter I had with a bright, young African-American man a few years ago comes to mind. He was raised in a Christian home but became convinced that the Bible condones slavery, racism, and other repugnant ideas. Eventually, he abandoned the Bible as outdated and immoral by contemporary standards. Decades (and even centuries) of Christians using the Bible to justify such ugly practices didn't help matters.

We sat down together for hours and wrestled with the Bible's difficult passages that seem (and only seem) to condone slavery. Those passages are laced with Eastern idioms that are unfamiliar or even off-putting to Western ears. But when properly understood, the harshness gives way to something ennobling and valuable for people of all races. It is, of course, true that imperialists have used Christianity to oppress others. Avarice-enchanted men contorted Christianity to rationalize the slave trade, conquests of indigenous peoples, and forced conversions. At times, Christians who didn't condone racism have turned a blind eye to it. But it was Christianity rightly understood and applied that brought about abolition and emancipation.

A famous abolitionist image that seared itself onto British retinas and hearts depicted an African slave kneeling as he asked the question, "Am I not a man and a brother?" This question eventually elicited white Britons to answer yes, because they were influenced by the olive-skinned gospel that declares all humans to be the bearers of God's very image. True, it took decades to accomplish. But it likely never would have been accomplished were it not for the message of equality so profoundly uttered and demonstrated by the brown-eyed and woolly-haired Jesus.

The young man I spoke with was beginning to see the Bible's Easternness and how it impacted Europe for the better. In other words, he had seen that the cultural current about the evils of Western, imperialist Christianity could and perhaps should be resisted after all. Seeing Jesus from the East is critical for Westerners, whose culture owes so much to the carpenter from Nazareth.

The critic may say that the problem with Christianity is that the Bible can equally be used to justify racial oppression and gender discrimination as it can to champion equal rights. This is simply not the case. Indeed, secular and atheistic thinkers have concluded that it requires quite a bit of textual and mental gymnastics to get the Bible to justify oppression and discrimination. As we will see, freedom and equality—values championed by Western civilization today—drip ripely from the vines of Scripture. From the beginning of Scripture's pages we see that Christianity is not inherently a Western imperialist religion.

BACK TO THE FUTURE WITH THE OLIVE-SKINNED GOSPEL

To see if we should swim against the narrative current that labels Christianity as a white imperialist religion, we need to traverse another stream—the stream of time. Like Marty McFly, we'll travel back farther and farther before returning to modern times. "Middle Eastern Christians have been called the forgotten faithful," Kenneth Bailey writes.[1] When many people think of Christianity, they think of European cathedrals or oak-laden and stained glass–ornamented American churches. While that's common to Christianity's Western trappings, Westerners shouldn't ignore the gospel's original Middle Easternness.

I recall a humorous exchange told to me by an American pastor. His church had just begun exploring how it might help foster peace in the Middle East, so he was meeting with Israelis and Arabs. He had the pleasure of meeting a wonderful Palestinian pastor from Bethlehem. Assuming that the Palestinian pastor had converted to Christianity from Islam, the American asked him, "So I'd love to hear your journey of faith. When did you convert to Christianity?" With a wry smile, the Palestinian pastor responded, "My family's Christian heritage goes back to the second century. We're the originals." And with a wink, he asked the American pastor, "When did *you guys* convert?" The American pastor was simultaneously amused and embarrassed, having been reminded that olive oil coursed through the early church's veins.

Kenneth Bailey, who spent so much of his life living in the Middle East, writes, "Arabic-speaking Christianity began on the day of Pentecost when some of those present heard the preaching of Peter in Arabic. In the early centuries, Arabic-speaking Christianity is known to have been widespread in the Yemen, Bahrain, Qatar and elsewhere."[2] When we forget that Jesus spoke and ministered in the context of a Middle Eastern culture, we can easily misjudge him by modern Western idioms and customs. Placing Jesus' words and deeds within an Eastern culture, where community identity and conformity far outweigh individual identity and expression, brings clarity and newfound relevance that we can benefit from today. In the preceding chapters, we hope you've seen the sights, smelled the aromas, heard the expressions, and tasted the flavors of that context.

But there's more than just clarity to be gained. While Jesus was thoroughly Middle Eastern, his actions formed the core of later Western values. He bucked tradition and authority to upend the injustices endemic to his culture. Interestingly, those same injustices persist in our day, nearly two thousand years later and thousands of miles away. Seeing Jesus' Easternness brings not only fresh clarity; seeing Jesus as the Eastern bridge to Western culture also brings hope as we struggle in the West to address the same issues he dealt with so long ago.

JESUS THE ANTI-TRIBALIST

Many critics argue that religion, specifically Middle Eastern monotheisms, has led to ignorance, superstition, and tribalism that hold back human progress. For these folks, logic, reason, and science, presumably championed in the Western Enlightenment, will save us once again. Somehow the irony of this argument has escaped these critics. They decry faith traditions like Christianity as imperialistic tools of Western aggression that keep people in ignorance, but then they want to impose purportedly Western Enlightenment values on the non-Western world. Easterners (yes, even ancient Easterners) regularly employed reason, logic, and science to their daily lives without needing Europeans to tell them to do so.

It's true that Easterners have a story-driven, circuitous way of applying logic, but they apply it with the same force as anyone else. To say that Westerners have a lock on logic, truth, and discovery is the height of arrogance. "All the intelligent people were not born in the twentieth century," writes Bailey. Describing the timeless wisdom and ingenious prose in the Bible, he says, "When we observe these sophisticated, thoughtful and artistically balanced rhetorical styles, we form a high opinion of their authors."[3]

The implied dichotomy between Western Enlightenment and Eastern religiosity leads to an "us versus them" tribalism, which atheistic champions of Enlightenment-age values such as Steven Pinker want to end. That's a further irony—pitting Western values against Eastern tribalism is, well, tribalistic.

We should be especially sensitive to this kind of tribalism in our day when everything is so polarized. Every political event is charged with animosity toward "the other side." Free speech is violently stifled by those claiming to be freedom's champions. It's easy to label someone a "hater" rather than debate ideas. Judicial confirmation hearings have become tribalized circuses.

Jesus spoke and acted in no less of a tribal culture. The Middle East of the first century was divided along racial and ethnic lines. It was also strongly divided along gender lines. Those of different religious bents were often at odds with each other. And politics was an ever-pervasive source of division and derision. In other words, Jesus' culture was curiously similar to our own.

That's why Jesus' way of turning situations on their heads can help us today. His ancient wisdom surprises us again and again in how contemporary it actually is. Marcello Pera, the atheist philosopher and former Italian politician, has argued powerfully that Western love of liberty, equality, and brotherhood simply wouldn't exist without the Christian message.[4]

JESUS, RACE, AND ETHNICITY

As I think about how Jesus addressed racial and ethnic tensions that are similar to what we deal with today, his encounter with a Gentile (non-Jewish) woman leaps to mind (Matthew 15:21–28). In fact, she wasn't just a Gentile; she was a Canaanite—the very people who had committed such atrocities against the Hebrews that God commanded their very way of life to be wiped out (Deuteronomy 7:20; Joshua 11; Judges 1:2).

The context of this encounter is key. Jesus went to Tyre and Sidon, which today are in modern Lebanon. The Canaanite woman called Jesus the "Son of David" (verse 22)—a specifically Jewish way of referring to the Messiah—and asked him to help her demon-oppressed daughter. The cultural and religious norms of the day called for Jews to ignore Gentile pleas. In fact, Jesus' disciples begged him to send her away (verse 23). Jesus used the situation not only to help the woman, but also to teach people—especially his own disciples—to overcome their prejudices.

Merely saying something like "God loves everybody, regardless of ethnicity" wouldn't have stuck in the Middle Eastern mind. The Middle East has always been so awash in idioms and platitudes that such a statement would have been diluted. Middle Easterners love clever banter, however, and that's what sticks. So Jesus engaged the woman in exactly that.

At first, Jesus seemed to rebuff her plea with silence, seeming to conform to cultural expectations. He then built on this by surfacing the ethnic division between her and him. "I was sent only to the lost sheep of Israel," he told her (verse 24). But she was undaunted, persisting even to the point of calling Jesus "Lord." Jesus had a point to make to both Jews and Canaanites who gathered around to watch the spectacle. With a sarcastic tone meant to ferret out the prejudices of the very people listening, Jesus aped the Jewish-centered response the crowd expected. "It is not right to take the children's bread and toss it to the dogs" (verse 26). Savvy enough to see where Jesus was heading, the woman quipped back, "Yes, Lord, yet even the dogs eat the crumbs that fall from their masters' table" (verse 27 ESV).

"O woman, great is your faith!" he exclaimed. "Be it done for you as you desire" (verse 28 ESV).[5] Jesus healed her daughter and honored the faith of the Canaanite woman, whose motherly love gave her the courage to breach ethnic and religious barriers. He involved her in the lesson to the crowd. He wasn't interested in only removing the demon that oppressed the woman's daughter, but also in exorcising the demon of racism that had oppressed Israel, Canaan, and the entire region.

This wasn't an isolated incident. At another time, a Roman centurion asked Jesus to heal his servant and Jesus obliged. Again Jesus praised the faith of a non-Jew: "I tell you, not even in Israel have I found such faith" (Luke 7:9 ESV).

In these two examples (among several others) Jesus highlighted the faith of non-Jews before those mired in the ethnocentric religiosity around him. The master of paradox, he upended tradition to effectuate change.

In stark contrast to what we see happening today, Jesus wasn't interested in catering to "his base" or "his side." He wanted to rectify social wrongs while teaching people.

He coupled his message with action. His words and his deeds healed cultural divides and individual people. Perhaps we in the modern West could learn something from this timeless Easterner.

I realize that simply appealing to Christian beliefs won't go far enough toward dissipating and resolving the racial tensions that beset us today. Commonality of belief doesn't automatically result in seeing and striving for the common good. But Jesus' teaching and his actions make him the eternally contemporary example of what it takes to move beyond shallow talk of commonality. Indeed, Jesus consistently spent time with those who were considered ethnically "questionable" or compromised by his society. Yet he upheld their basic dignity and included them in the kingdom of God, should they choose to follow and rely on him. One need only delve into the moving story in John 4 of Jesus' encounter with the Samaritan woman and her entire village to see how he bridges ethnic divides.

Most importantly, Jesus established self-sacrifice as the chief means of harmony and reconciliation. He gave his life for Jew and Gentile, Ethiopian and Roman, man and woman. His is a radical example to follow, especially today, when self-sacrifice for the good of someone who stands outside our perceived tribe is in short supply.

Yet a strong and strident criticism remains: neither Jesus nor his apostles seem to have condemned the worst form of racism of all—slavery. "Sure," a skeptic may argue "Jesus and his followers talked about unity and the like, but they never put their money where their mouths were. They never stood up to the Roman slavery system, and they didn't condemn the Old Testament's seeming endorsement of slavery." So what real, practical good is all this talk about ethnic and racial reconciliation and equality?

In addition to some of the initial thoughts Ravi and I have shared in the pages of this book, I intend to write specifically and in greater detail on the subject of Jesus and slavery soon. Others have offered thoughtful responses to this objection as well. Suffice it to say for now that as far as the Old Testament's supposed condoning of slavery, brilliant minds have demonstrated that "slavery" in the Bible is not to be understood in the same sense as modern-day slavery, the Western European slave trade, or the slavery of the antebellum American South. Slavery of that kind may be described in the Bible, but it is nowhere condoned.[6] Rather, what the Bible describes as permissible for ancient Israel was a form of indentured servitude, a voluntary situation that was meant to be temporary until a person's debt was paid. That's why, when confronting the much different Roman system, *the apostle Paul expressly called chattel slavery a sin* (see 1 Timothy 1:10). Though it didn't do so perfectly, the early church tried to change hearts to bring about changes in oppressive political systems that violate the uniquely Judeo-Christian belief that all people are created in God's image (Genesis 1:26–27).

For example, Paul took the spiritual reality of human equality before God and applied it to worldly situations. He modeled real change in word and deed. Paul wrote to a fellow Christian named Philemon about how he ought to forgive the debt owed by a runaway slave named Onesimus. In fact, Paul went so far as to offer to take the runaway slave's place, urging Philemon to count Onesimus's debt against Paul. Paul owed

Philemon nothing—in fact Philemon owed Paul—but Paul willingly took on the slave's debt. In that sense, he redeemed Onesimus, reflecting the way Jesus had redeemed Paul himself (Philemon 17–21). Paul sought to free Onesimus the slave from economic bondage while simultaneously setting Philemon, the slave owner, free from his immoral chains.

It worked. In a later letter, we learn that Paul sent Onesimus to Colossae with Tychicus to give everyone there an update on how the gospel was spreading. "I have sent him [Tychicus] to you for this very purpose, that you may know how we are and that he may encourage your hearts," Paul writes, "and with him Onesimus, our faithful and beloved brother, *who is one of you*" (Colossians 4:8–9 ESV, emphasis mine). Onesimus, the runaway slave, returned to Colossae as an equal.

I have often wondered why the New Testament book of Philemon, a short personal letter in which Paul is simply trying to settle a dispute between two people, swells the pages of Holy Writ's sweeping saga. Perhaps it's because this little letter demonstrates that mere propositional belief doesn't bring about change unless it is put into action.

That is a Middle Eastern perspective, after all. Westerners try to distill truths to practical, propositional statements. Middle Easterners latch onto truths through colorful stories and parables. Their illustrations are not rhetorical fluff; they are preservatives. Paul's short letter to Philemon is a parable come to living history. It illustrates what belief put to action can do.

Social reformers like William Wilberforce understood this, which is why he had two great aims: (1) the abolition of the slave trade and (2) the reformation of manners (or morality). England at the time was beset with debauched living and terrible public vices. Criminals were hanged and burned publicly, among other abhorrent behavior. Wilberforce and his friends of the Clapham Sect sought to change hearts and minds by turning them back to the gospel. Then barbaric laws could also be changed. Wilberforce's Western efforts were inspired by the Middle Eastern Jesus and Paul, both of whom knew that laws can change when hearts change.

Ethnic and racial equality were startling ideas to the Middle Eastern mind in Jesus' and Paul's time. It is fashionable to think of those in the ancient Near East as backward racists, yet in the twenty-first century, we still find the idea of racial equality difficult to implement. One wonders if we've ever really done the about-face that would deem the ancients backward and us forward-looking. Scripture was progressive when it was written, and it is just as progressive today. Perhaps we should lay down our modern cockiness and allow ourselves to be surprised by the Bible once more.

JESUS AND GENDER EQUALITY

In the very early days of my ministry, I walked through the halls of a university building after giving a nerve-racking talk. My hosts were taking me to a display put up by the Secular Student Alliance. It was quite fascinating. Books like Sam Harris's *The End of Faith* and Richard Dawkins's *The God Delusion* were shown, with a plaque next to them that read, "**TRUTH**" in bold lettering. The Bible was also on display, but with a plaque that read, **"FALSE"** next to it. The display included Bible passages taken out of context that seemed to promote misogyny, raping of women, and treating them like property. The display not only swam in the Western cultural narrative that Christianity is a white, male religion that oppresses women, but it was also trying to hurry that current along.

It was an appallingly superficial treatment of the Bible—a terrible example of quote mining to fit a predefined narrative. Of course, the Bible has been misused by some men to justify treating women as second-class citizens. I daresay, however, that the Bible properly understood contains not only a few gems of passages and stories about the equality of women, but full treasure troves of teachings, laws, and accounts about women's status as those who bear God's image equally to men. Exploring that trove will help us swim against the cultural stream.[7]

In the Christian tradition, the single most important event in human history is Jesus' resurrection. The resurrection proved Jesus right in his claim that humanity is sinfully separated from God, that he himself could bridge the chasm between God and humanity by paying the debt we deserved to pay, and that he had power over death—humanity's seemingly invincible enemy. The Bible records that the first people to lay eyes on Jesus' resurrected body were women. This isn't a mere scrap of narrative detail. In the first-century Middle East, a woman's testimony was worth half that of a man, if it was worth anything at all. Yet the gospel message that Jesus had risen from the dead was meant to take root in that very context.

This aspect of the Bible's account is of utmost importance for at least two reasons. First, it lends credibility to the resurrection narrative. Consider this: if the gospel writers (or the early church) had invented Jesus' resurrection, would they have made women the first eyewitnesses to the fact? No, they would have made men the heroes and the witnesses. Choosing women as the first eyewitnesses would have been laughable to the Middle Eastern mind, making the account less acceptable. The gospel authors would have had no incentive to write that account—unless that's how it actually happened.

Second, and just as important, Jesus seemed to be making a statement about the character, quality, and value of women by honoring them as the primary witnesses to his crowning miracle. The Middle Eastern mind-set of that day discounted their value. I daresay Jesus' own disciples likely did that same thing before the resurrection. Yet Jesus chose women not only to be the first to see him risen, but also to tell the men what had happened. How poetic! Jesus used the misogyny of his day to simultaneously give credible evidence of his resurrection and to turn the tables on his culture's devaluing of women.

So much more could be said. There are concrete examples throughout the pages of Holy Writ demonstrating gender equality:

- The Bible counts women among the prophets who spoke for God, specifically identifying five and alluding to many more not specifically listed (Exodus 15:20; Judges 4–5; 2 Kings 22:14; Nehemiah 6:14; Isaiah 8:3; Luke 2:36; Acts 21:9).

- God elevated Deborah to the position of "judge," a leader with authority over the most highly placed men in Israel (Judges 4–5).
- God heard the plea of Hagar and promised to provide for her and her son as they despaired in the desert (Genesis 16:7–14).
- When a prostitute showed the kind of integrity needed to advance God's plan, she was saved from judgment and is specifically named among the heroes of faith in the book of Hebrews (Hebrews 11:31).
- When King Josiah found the Book of the Law, he directed a woman named Huldah to verify it (2 Kings 22:14).
- Books of the Bible such as Ruth and Esther bear the names of women of courage and integrity.

The Bible's recognition of the dignity of women has echoed down through the centuries. Some time ago, I was in Manhattan for media interviews and meetings, staying at a hotel near Times Square. My fitness tracking watch admonished me to get my steps in, so I ventured outside, and the walk afforded me an opportunity to people watch. As I strolled around, my eyes were barraged with garish, high-definition billboards; my ears were assaulted by hucksters trying to sell me tickets to stand-up comedy shows; and my nostrils inhaled the smells coming from the booths of innumerable food vendors on every corner. Through the sensory overload I beheld some interesting juxtapositions.

Various street performers dressed like the Statue of Liberty and superheroes, and others dressed in equally eye-catching costumes, offered to have their pictures taken with tourists. I couldn't help but notice four particular performers in the midst of the throng. They were women, barely clothed, offering to have their pictures taken with men for money. It was shocking to say the least—and all in plain view of children eager to storm the massive M&M and Disney stores in Times Square.

As I averted my gaze and paced through the crowd, I couldn't help but wonder, *Who is the more debased—the women offering themselves or the men who take them up on it?* I also saw Muslim families, some of the women with covered heads and even covered faces. Again, I couldn't help but wonder, *What do these two different kinds of women think of each other? Do the barely clothed women consider themselves to be liberated and free while thinking that the hijab-adorned Muslim women are oppressed by religion? Do the Muslim women lament the fact that the performers are so willing to use their bodies as commodities to make a buck? And what about everyone else who passed by, seeing both the unclad and the fully draped? Did they even give a moment's pause to reflect on the human contradictions?*

Contrast that scene with the elderly Asian woman I saw in Times Square later that evening. She was standing at a busy street corner, gazing up and holding a sign with the simple message, "Jesus loves you—John 3:16." She silently stood there with a compassionate look on her face as the crowds parted around her like a river flowing around a boulder. She saw the inherent dignity in *every* human being, a dignity offered to the women and to the men.

Feminine dignity cannot truly be secured by flesh peddling, nor by religiously imposed modesty. The ideal of feminine dignity, so elusive for us even today, has been secured by the Middle Eastern man from Nazareth. His words expressed dignity for women. His actions imparted status to those whom society tried to suppress. As male Easterners beheld this Jesus, they were challenged and taught to overcome their prejudices. As Eastern women spent time with him, they rediscovered the original dignity they had been conditioned to forget. As we in the West look on Jesus now, perhaps we can move forward and better grasp a future laced with equality of race and gender by peering through time and seeing Jesus from the East.

JESUS—THE FAMILIAR NOVELTY

How amazing that Jesus' Easternness is what so beautifully addresses Western issues today. When his actions and words are understood within an Eastern context, Western eyes can behold Jesus' Easternness as novel, yet timeless. At the same time, Easterners who have been told Christianity is a tool of Western imperialism can recapture Jesus as one of them and thus behold him afresh.

When I beheld the power of salmon swimming up a mountain stream, I was awed beyond what any description of the phenomenon might inspire. Beholding how Jesus swims against the common narrative stream of being a Western God is even more awe-inspiring. His Easternness confounds our narratives, yet his ability to address the very issues that plague Western culture make him timelessly familiar to us all. He has influenced ancients and moderns. He has influenced the East and the West. We simply must give him a fresh look.

ACKNOWLEDGMENTS

This book, like so many, is really the product of many minds, not just those of the coauthors. In fact, the first mind to be involved in the creation of this book was our dear friend Nabeel Qureshi. He originally wanted to write this book with me (Ravi), based on our common experiences as Easterners living in the West and ministering around the globe. Upon his untimely passing, I thought it only fitting that Abdu, a former Muslim and a Middle Easterner who also lives in the West but traverses the globe, should help me carry Nabeel's vision forward.

I (Abdu) was honored that Ravi thought of me and jumped at the chance to complete a project so near to Nabeel's heart. Within minutes of talking with Ravi, I called Michelle Qureshi, Nabeel's widow, to ask if she would give me permission to fill in for him. I didn't need to ask permission but felt that doing so would give the proper honor and respect to both of them. I'm grateful that she so unhesitatingly allowed me to participate in this project. Ravi and I pray that this book honors her as much as it does her husband.

RAVI ZACHARIAS

My wife, Margie, worked very hard on this book, and so my greatest thanks go to her. Editing my work is not easy. I write just as I speak. Sometimes there are chasms of thought that are leaped over. She is the one who knows my thinking the best and is able to follow how I got to where I did. So my heartfelt thanks to her. The same applies to Danielle DuRant, my research assistant for more than a quarter of a century. I have said many times that if I forget where I said something, she knows exactly where to find it. The fact is, as the years go by, we realize how much of our accuracy is dependent on others who work with us. Margie and Danielle have been of stellar value in my writings.

My thanks also to Zondervan for trusting me with this theme. They are a great publisher, and I am honored to work with their assigned team.

Finally, to RZIM and Abdu. RZIM gives me the time to get away and write. Abdu has been a delight to work with.

ABDU MURRAY

I'm grateful for the efforts of Randy Pistor, who has selflessly helped me with research along the way, as he has with other projects as well. My good friends Joe Mastro and Brandon Cleaver reviewed chapters and helped me work through some ideas, and Carson Weitnauer provided valuable information on Western versions of shame culture. Their efforts undoubtedly improved the final product. My assistant, Tara Ehrhardt, always provides eager support and was similarly helpful in this endeavor. My wife, Nicole, provided a sounding board for various ideas and read each chapter with an eye toward the audience. But more than that, I'm thankful for her patience, which was so helpful on those occasions when I sat distracted at the dinner table, wrestling to get a thought out.

I am profoundly grateful to Ravi Zacharias for inviting me to help him with this book and for years of mentorship and serving as an example of what it looks like to see Jesus on this side of heaven. It is to Jesus himself that I am most grateful.

NOTES

Chapter 1: A Story, a Family, and a Son

1. Matthew Arnold, "Sohrab and Rustum: An Episode," in *Matthew Arnold's Sohrab and Rustum and Other Poems*, Justus Collins Castleman, ed. (New York: Macmillan, 1905), 1.
2. Abolqasem Ferdowsi, *The Shahnameh: The Persian Book of Kings* (New York: Penguin, 2007), 189.
3. Arnold, "Sohrab and Rustum," 18.
4. Søren Kierkegaard, *Papers and Journals: A Selection* (New York: Penguin, 1996), 161.
5. See Paul Tillich, *Theology of Culture* (New York: Oxford University Press, 1959).
6. John Oxenham, "In Christ There Is No East or West" (1908).
7. Mahatma Gandhi, *Truth Is God: Gleanings from the Writings of Mahatma Gandhi Bearing on God, God Realization and the Godly Way* (Ahmedabad: Navajivan Trust, 1955), 14.
8. Oscar Wilde, *The Collected Works of Oscar Wilde* (London: Wordsworth, 2007), 908.
9. Charles Wesley, "And Can It Be That I Should Gain" (1738).

Chapter 2: The Messenger and the Message

1. Rohit Kumar, "How Would Jesus Have Fared Amongst Contemporary Indian Godmen," *The Wire*, December 25,

231

2018, https://thewire.in/religion/how-would-jesus-have-fared-amongst-contemporary-indian-godmen.

2. Shared in a conversation with a friend who is a Christian from a Hindu background. His brother, an atheist skeptic, had set up this scenario to him.

3. See, for example, "bread of life" (6:35), "I Am" (8:58), and "the good shepherd" (10:14). There are many more in John.

4. Merrill Tenney, *John: The Gospel of Belief: An Analytic Study of the Text* (Grand Rapids: Eerdmans, 1948), 52.

5. See Francis Schaeffer, *He Is There and He Is Not Silent*, 30th anniv. ed. (Wheaton, IL: Tyndale, 2001).

6. Nicholas Wolterstorff, *Lament for a Son* (Grand Rapids: Eerdmans, 1987), 72–73.

Chapter 3: Lost and Found for All

1. Quoted in John Heilpern, "A Nice Coopa Tea with Alan Bennett," *Observer*, April 28, 2003, https://observer.com/2003/04/a-nice-coopa-tea-with-alan-bennett.

2. Jasmine Holmes, "Rethinking Apologetics for the Black Church," *Christianity Today*, July 18, 2018, www.christianitytoday.com/women/2018/july/rethinking-apologetics-for-black-church.html.

3. See Julia Belluz, "Is the CRISPR Baby Controversy the Start of a Terrifying New Chapter in Gene Editing?" *Vox*, January 22, 2019, www.vox.com/science-and-health/2018/11/30/18119589/crispr-gene-editing-he-jiankui.

4. Quoted in Josh Gabbatiss, "Gene-Edited Chinese Babies May Have 'Enhanced Brains,' Scientists Say," *The Independent*, February 22, 2019, www.independent.co.uk/news/science/gene-edited-baby-china-brain-intelligence-hiv-he-jiankui-crispr-a8792386.html.

5. Exact title and author unknown. Poem attributed to Harriet Flewelling, an acquaintance of Gladys Bliss, per correspondence on August 6, 2019.

Chapter 4: Honor, Shame, and Jesus

1. I've written about how emotional barriers and personal costs keep people—Western or Eastern, religious or secular—from objectively considering the strength of the evidence for a counter worldview in my book *Grand Central Question: Answering the Critical Concerns of the Major Worldviews* (Downers Grove, IL: InterVarsity, 2014), 13–28.

2. Simon Chan, *Grassroots Asian Theology: Thinking the Faith from the Ground Up* (Downers Grove, IL: IVP Academic, 2014), 83.

3. Juliet November, *Honor/Shame Cultures: A Beginner's Guide to Cross-Cultural Missions* (Amazon Kindle Direct Publishing, 2017), 16–17, italics original.

4. See November, *Honor/Shame Cultures*, 18.

5. For a detailed treatment of honor-shame cultures, see November, *Honor/Shame Cultures*; E. Randolph Richards and Brandon J. O'Brien, *Misreading Scripture with Western Eyes: Removing Cultural Blinders to Better Understand the Bible* (Downers Grove, IL: InterVarsity, 2012).

6. A more in-depth discussion of how honor and shame are illustrated through this story can be found in Richards and O'Brien, *Misreading Scripture*, 119–26.

7. Richards and O'Brien, *Misreading Scripture*, 129.

8. See Federal Rules of Evidence 2019 Edition, "Rule 801—Definitions That Apply to This Article; Exclusions from Hearsay," 801(c), www.rulesofevidence.org/article-viii/rule-801.

9. See Federal Rules of Evidence 2019 Edition, "Rule 804—Hearsay Exceptions; Declarant Unavailable," 804(b)(3), www.rulesofevidence.org/article-viii/rule-804/.

10. S. Radhakrishnan, *The Philosophy of Rabindranath Tagore* (London: Macmillan, 1918), 15.

11. See Ibn Kathir, *Tafsir of Ibn Kathir*, vol. 3 (New York: Darussalam, 2000), 25–27.

12. Tanith Carey, "Anne Darwin, 'Canoe Widow': 'Deceiving My Sons Was Unforgivable,'" *Guardian*, October 10, 2016, www.theguardian.com/lifeandstyle/2016/oct/08/anne -darwin-deceiving-my-sons-was-unforgivable.

13. Monica Lewinsky, "The Price of Shame" March 2015, at 13:25, 14:10, www.ted.com/talks/monica_lewinsky_the _price_of_shame.

14. Lewinsky, "The Price of Shame," at 5:00.

15. For an excellent and concise treatment of the biblical doctrine of atonement, see William Lane Craig, *The Atonement* (Cambridge: Cambridge University Press, 2018).

16. November, *Honor/Shame Cultures*, 17.

17. Isaac Watts, *The Psalms and Hymns of Isaac Watts*, Psalm 25, part 1, Christian Classics Ethereal Library, http://stlfasola .org/Watts_Psalms_And_Hymns.pdf.

Chapter 5: The Rewards of Sacrifice

1. Cited in Patrick Wintour, "Persecution of Christians 'Coming Close to Genocide' in Middle East—Report," *The Guardian*, May 2, 2019, www.theguardian.com/world/ 2019/may/02/persecution-driving-christians-out-of-middle -east-report.

2. Kenneth E. Bailey, *Jesus Through Middle Eastern Eyes: Cultural Studies in the Gospels* (Downers Grove, IL: InterVarsity, 2008), 68, italics original.

3. Bailey, *Jesus Through Middle Eastern Eyes*, 70.

4. C. S. Lewis, *The Problem of Pain* (New York: Macmillan, 1962), 93.

5. *Bible Sense Lexicon*, Logos Bible Software (Bellingham, WA: Faithlife, 2019), https://ref.ly/logos4/Senses?KeyId=ws.give +graciously.v.01.

6. Dallas Willard, *The Great Omission: Reclaiming Jesus's Essential Teachings on Discipleship* (San Francisco: HarperSan Francisco, 2006), 14.

7. Quoted in Russell Goldman, "Saudi Arabia's Beheading of a Nanny Followed Strict Procedures," *ABC News*, January 11, 2013, https://abcnews.go.com/US/saudi-arabias-beheading-nanny-strict-procedures/story?id=18182757.

Chapter 6: Parables

1. Richards and O'Brien, *Misreading Scripture*, 84, italics original.
2. Bailey, *Jesus Through Middle Eastern Eyes*, 280.
3. Bailey, *Jesus Through Middle Eastern Eyes*, 294.
4. Bailey, *Jesus Through Middle Eastern Eyes*, 296.
5. Bob Dufford, "Be Not Afraid" (copyright 1975, 1978 by Robert J. Dufford, SJ, and OCP).

Chapter 7: The Temple and the Wedding

1. George Croly, "Spirit of God, Descend Upon My Heart" (1854).
2. Thomas Merton, *The Seven Storey Mountain: An Autobiography of Faith* (New York: Harcourt, 1948), 246.
3. Frederic Weatherly, "The Holy City" (1892).
4. See C. S. Lewis, *The Four Loves* (1960; repr., New York: Harcourt, 1991) and his chapters "Affection," "Friendship," "Eros," and "Charity," pp. 31–141.
5. Ravi Zacharias, *Has Christianity Failed You?* (Grand Rapids: Zondervan, 2010).
6. John Keble, "The Voice That Breathed O'er Eden" (1857).

Chapter 8: The Temptation and the Transfiguration

1. Michel Quoist, *Prayers* (Lanham, MD: Rowman & Littlefield, 1999), 135. Used by permission of Rowman & Littlefield Publishing Group. All rights reserved.
2. For the accounts of the temptation of Christ in the Gospels, see Matthew 4:1–11; Mark 1:12–13; Luke 4:1–13.
3. See Thomas Chalmers, "The Expulsive Power of a New Affection," Christianity.com, March 2, 2010, www

.christianity.com/christian-life/spiritual-growth/the-expulsive-power-of-a-new-affection-11627257.html.

4. Arthur Leonard Griffith, *God's Time and Ours: Sermons for Festivals and Seasons of the Christian Year* (Nashville: Abingdon, 1964), 76.

5. For the three accounts of the transfiguration of Christ in the Gospels, see Matthew 17:1–8; Mark 9:2–8; Luke 9:28–36.

6. Fanny J. Crosby, "To God Be the Glory" (1875).

7. Alexander Pope (1688–1744), *The Dunciad: Book IV*, lines 649–656, https://rpo.library.utoronto.ca/poems/dunciad-book-iv.

8. Arthur Hugh Clough, "Say Not, the Struggle Nought Availeth," in *Selected Poems*, ed. Shirley Chew (New York: Routledge, 2003), 58.

Chapter 9: Why Should Westerners Care How Easterners See Jesus?

1. Bailey, *Jesus Through Middle Eastern Eyes*, 11.

2. Bailey, *Jesus Through Middle Eastern Eyes*, 12.

3. Bailey, *Jesus Through Middle Eastern Eyes*, 18.

4. Marcello Pera, "How Necessary Is Christianity to European Identity?" January 26, 2011, http://marcellopera.it/index.php/it/sala-stampa/interventi/840-how-necessary-is-christianity-to-european-identity.

5. Kenneth Bailey provides a masterful and detailed explanation of this encounter in *Jesus Through Middle Eastern Eyes*, 217–26.

6. For thoughtful and in-depth discussions, I recommend Paul Copan, *Is God a Moral Monster? Making Sense of the Old Testament God* (Grand Rapids: Baker, 2011).

7. Again, like the issue of race and Christianity, I intend to write more extensively on the issue of women and the Bible in a forthcoming book.

Seeing Jesus from the East Video Study

A Fresh Look at History's Most Influential Figure

Ravi Zacharias and Abdu Murray

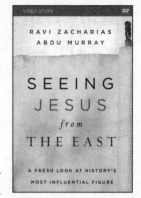

Today, our world is growing smaller through advances in travel and communication. And as West meets East, we are becoming more aware of the cultural assumptions we each bring to our interpretation of the Bible. In many Western cultures, Jesus is seen primarily through the lens of Western reasoning and linear thought. Western readers often miss the underlying nuances in the text that reflect the Eastern mind-set of the authors of Scripture.

In the *Seeing Jesus from the East Video Study*, a companion to the *Seeing Jesus from the East* book and the *Seeing Jesus from the East Study Guide*, Ravi Zacharias and Abdu Murray show us why a broader view of Jesus is needed. They capture a revitalized gospel message through an Eastern lens, revealing its power afresh and sharing the truth about Jesus in a compelling and winsome light. Incorporating story, vivid imagery, and the concepts of honor and shame, sacrifice, and rewards, the *Seeing Jesus from the East Video Study* equips you for a fresh encounter with the living and boundless Jesus.

Saving Truth

Finding Meaning and Clarity in a Post-Truth World

Abdu Murray

Increasingly, Western culture embraces confusion as a virtue and decries certainty as a sin. Those who are confused about sexuality and identity are viewed as heroes. Those who are confused about morality are progressive pioneers. Those who are confused about spirituality are praised as tolerant. Conversely, those who express certainty about any of these issues are seen as bigoted, oppressive, arrogant, or intolerant.

This cultural phenomenon led the compilers of the *Oxford English Dictionary* to name "post-truth" their 2016 "Word of the Year." How can Christians offer truth and clarity to a world that shuns both?

By accurately describing the culture of confusion and how it has affected our society, Abdu Murray seeks to awaken Westerners to the plight we find ourselves in. He also challenges Christians to consider how they have played a part in fostering this culture through bad arguments, unwise labeling, and emotional attacks.

Ultimately, *Saving Truth* provides arguments from a Christian perspective for the foundations of truth and how these foundations apply to sexuality, identity, morality, and spirituality. For those enmeshed in the culture of confusion, the book offers a way to untangle oneself and find hope in the clarity that Christ offers.

Available in stores and online!

ZONDERVAN®
.com

The Grand Weaver

How God Shapes Us Through the Events of Our Lives

Ravi Zacharias

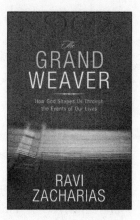

How differently would we live if we believed that every dimension of our lives—from the happy to the tragic to the mundane—were part of a beautiful and purposeful design in which no threads were wrongly woven? That's what bestselling author and internationally known apologist Ravi Zacharias explores in *The Grand Weaver.*

As Christians, we believe that great events, such as a death or a birth, are guided by the hand of God. Yet we drift into feeling that our daily lives are the product of our own efforts. This book brims with penetrating stories and insights that show us otherwise. From a chance encounter in a ticket line to a beloved father's final words before dying, from a random phone call to a line in a Scripture reading, every detail of life is woven into its perfect place. In *The Grand Weaver*, Ravi examines our backgrounds, our disappointments, our triumphs, and our beliefs and explains how they are all part of the intentional and perfect work of the Grand Weaver.

Available in stores and online!

The End of Reason

A Response to the New Atheists

Ravi Zacharias

When you pray, are you talking to a God who exists? Or is God nothing more than your "imaginary friend," like a playmate contrived by a lonely and imaginative child?

When author Sam Harris attacked Christianity in *Letter to a Christian Nation*, reviewers called the book "marvelous," and a generation of readers—hundreds of thousands of them—were drawn to his message. Deeply troubled, Dr. Ravi Zacharias knew he had to respond. In *The End of Reason*, Zacharias underscores the dependability of the Bible, along with his belief in the power and goodness of God. He confidently refutes Harris's claims that God is nothing more than a figment of one's imagination and that Christians regularly practice intolerance and hatred around the globe.

If you found Harris's book compelling, *The End of Reason* is exactly what you need. Ravi exposes "the utter bankruptcy of this worldview." And if you haven't read Harris's book, Ravi's response remains a powerful, passionate, irrefutably sound set of arguments for Christian thought. The clarity and hope in these pages reach out to readers who know and follow God, as well as to those who reject God.

Available in stores and online!